TECHNIQUES OF ACTING

TECHNIQUES OF ACTING

BY RONALD HAYMAN

HOLT, RINEHART AND WINSTON
New York/Chicago/San Francisco

ISBN: 0–03–086708–8
Library of Congress Catalog Card Number: 70–155514
First published in the United States 1971

Printed in the United States of America

FOR MONICA

CONTENTS

ACKNOWLEDGEMENTS

A full list of the books and publications referred to in the text is given at the back of this book. In particular, the author is indebted to the BBC, to Vanessa Redgrave, Dame Edith Evans, Dame Sybil Thorndike, Sir Laurence Olivier, Sir John Gielgud and Albert Finney and to Michael MacOwan and Michael Elliott for permission to quote extracts from BBC television interviews.

For in every action what is principally intended by the doer, whether he acts of natural necessity or voluntarily, is the clarification of his own image. Thus it is that every doer, to the extent of his doing, delights in it, for everything that is desires its own being; and since in doing the doer's being is somehow amplified, delight necessarily follows . . . Nothing therefore acts unless it may thereby manifest whatever it is.

DANTE

TECHNIQUES OF ACTING

1 · A SKETCH MAP OF THE AREA

In England today we tend to be smug about our actors, claiming them as the best in the world. If this is true and if it is also true that every audience gets the acting it deserves, it follows that our audiences deserve more than any other audiences.

Whether this comfortable assumption is justified or not, I am convinced that our audiences could be much better than they are. The actor is just as much of a technician as the bull-fighter and, as in the bull-ring, an audience can only be appreciative of technical prowess if it is conscious and critical of technical faults. The ideal audience is not the naïve one which believes so hard in the characters and the story that it is unaware of the actors; the more aware it is of what they are doing, the better it is to play to. In the theatre, actors have an immediate sense of audience reaction and though, to some extent, they can control it, it also partly controls them. In television and cinema acting, there is no such two-way traffic, but actors still work, moment by moment, to a half-conscious idea of how audiences will react to what they are doing and the one sure way to raise the standard of film and television acting is to raise the standard of the audiences.

Not long ago it was considered dangerous to analyse the process of acting: if an actor discussed the secrets of his craft with his audience, he might offend his Muse and lose his inspiration. Something of this superstition has survived into a period in which no one believes in inspiration and to talk seriously about acting technique you still have to penetrate through a smokescreen of vagueness. No one even seems able to say what the technical differences are between acting for the stage, for films and for television. The word *technique* figures a lot in conversations about acting but actors themselves do not always know what they mean by it. Even in drama schools, where there are classes in 'Technique', the teachers are usually uncertain of what it is that they are teaching. They may be good at pointing out technical mistakes and laying down general rules like 'Always close a door with your upstage hand' but the endemic vagueness that bedevils all discussion of acting is reflected in the fact that we have not got a precise vocabulary or notation for it.

My attempts at clarification are intended equally for actors and audiences and it is probably best to start from the basic question of what exactly it is that an actor does. He does not appear to be doing anything different on stage or in front of the cameras from what we are all doing all the time. He talks, moves about, listens, smokes, laughs, goes out of the room, and the better his technique is, the more natural and spontaneous his behaviour seems. We all know perfectly well that every word he speaks has been learned from a script and every movement he makes rehearsed with a director but if he is any good, he persuades us into forgetting that he is moving along prepared lines towards a foregone conclusion. It must almost seem possible that this Othello will not kill this Desdemona at this performance. At the very least, we want to be surprised by his moods and his movements, even if we know every word he is going to speak. An actor who is predictable is a bad actor. A good actor, like a good poker player, keeps us on the alert, never sure of what he is going to do next. There was one style of acting in which the technique consisted partly in illustrating each word with a gesture and you still find a few old-fashioned actors who cannot talk about love without clapping their hands to their hearts, cannot say they are tired without yawning, cannot mention the sky without looking upwards. The actors who make us watch them are the actors who tell us something with their movements that we do not get simply from listening to the lines.

Off-stage, there are no technical problems involved in sitting in an armchair doing nothing. But in front of an audience, or a camera, it is impossible to relax without technique. Bad actors, both amateur and professional, behave in a totally artificial way. You can see them 'acting', self-consciously imitating what they have seen actors doing, but unable to hide their awareness of the audience and their intention of making a particular effect on it. Apart from the muscular and nervous tensions that afflict them in ordinary life, now that they are faced with the yawning black hollow of an auditorium or the inhuman eye of a camera, they cannot help showing that they are worried what they look like. Is my head too much in profile? Am I looking down too much? What did I do with my hands during rehearsals?

Much of the technical knowledge that an actor needs has to be assimilated so deeply that it becomes instinctive. Some lucky actors start off with natural confidence, natural physical relaxation, a well-placed voice, good diction, well co-ordinated movements and a good instinct for finding the right positions and angles on stage. Others, potentially just as good, may be much more dependent on drama school training to develop their basic talent and to teach them the essential principles. You[1] cannot act unless you know them but you cannot act until you no longer have to think about them, just as you cannot drive a car so long as you have to ask yourself exactly what movements you must go through with your hands and feet in order to change gear.

For instance you get into the habit of finding positions on stage where your eyes can turn to look at the other actors without turning away from the audience, where you are not partly masked by the other actors or by the furniture, where you leave yourself enough space for the movements you have to make without cramping yourself or anyone else, but you

---

[1] I am conscious of wanting to address both actors and audiences with the same 'you'. This seems right because a non-actor will only achieve a sympathetic understanding of the actor's problems if he imagines himself in the actor's shoes,

no longer think of your reasons for needing to be in this position. You learn how to cut your movements down to a meaningful minimum so as to avoid seeming fidgety and how to make them visible, without seeming to demonstrate them. Most of your face remains visible to the audience for most of the time but you no longer need to remind yourself about looking downstage. It becomes second nature to use your upstage hand for all possible business and you develop a feeling for when you need to move close to a particular character to adopt a particular tone with him and when it is better to have a wide space or a chair or some other obstacle in the way. You get to know how to time lines in relation to moves, when to pick up cues quickly, how to build towards a laugh that comes after someone else's line, how to vary your pace (and how pace is something quite different from speed), how to draw attention by moving and how to hold attention by stillness, how to avoid distracting the audience's attention during other actors' lines, how to make the most of an entrance or an exit and how to speak a line before an upstage exit without either saying it on the move with your back to the audience or speaking it downstage and leaving yourself with no line to cover your move up to the door. You learn which pauses add to theatrical tension and which destroy it, how to avoid picking up another actor's rhythm, how to space lines in order to give the audience time to focus on a visual reaction, how much – or how little – you need to look other actors in the eye. You learn various tricks to point reactions, like looking away from someone immediately before a 'take' which consists of looking in at him directly; or being involved in some action, so that just by interrupting or altering the rhythm of what you are doing you can indicate your reaction to something else.

All these are considerations which do not enter into normal behaviour off-stage and which may not have to enter consciously into behaviour on it. Certainly, any actor who concentrates on points like these is acting badly. But any good actor will not be dependent on his director for guidance on such basic matters, and he will also know when moves or business that the director gives him are going to create technical problems.

There is technique in using space; there is also technique in filling it. The object of voice training is to increase the range and flexibility of an actor's voice, to give him a maximum of control over both his breathing and how he spends his breath. It should enable him to be heard at the back of the gallery without seeming to raise his voice above the level he uses in ordinary life, though in fact he will be using more variation in volume, pitch, pace, tone and intensity. Training is as much a matter of learning what not to do as what to do. You have to avoid tension in the throat muscles, which produces hoarseness and loss of voice; you have to avoid characterizing by 'putting on' a false voice. But the well-trained voice will do what is required of it without specific briefing from the brain. Both in adapting to the technical requirements of a particular medium or a particular theatre and in shaping itself to a characterization.

Paul Scofield has described how this happened to him in his characterization of Sir Thomas More in Robert Bolt's *A Man for All Seasons*.[1] In finding out how More would feel, he found out how he would sound and he discovered that by using vocal characteristics he had never used before, he could make him sound mild even when the lines he was speaking were not mild.

> I used an accent for More that was absolutely a bastard thing of my own. My parents are Midland people, with a very regional accent, and I drew somewhat on this accent and mixed it with some others. The way More sounded just came out of my characterization of him as a lawyer. His dryness of mind, I thought, led him to use a sort of

[1] For details of this performance and others mentioned subsequently, see Appendix I, page 171.

dryness of speech. It evolved as I evolved the character. I would flatten or elongate a vowel in a certain way to get a certain effect . . . Because you're thinking and feeling all these things, the voice comes out in a certain way.[1]

The amount of projection needed varies enormously from role to role and from theatre to theatre, according to the size and shape of the auditorium, and how full it is, and even according to the mood of the audience. Ideally, none of the adaptations necessary should be conscious ones, but after a long run in a small theatre, it can be very difficult to re-tailor a performance to fit a large one. In the production of Jack Gelber's play *The Connection*, which came to the Duke of York's from a very small off-Broadway theatre, Warren Finnerty and Garry Goodrow were both outstanding but they were doing the right things on the wrong scale. Both performances were sincere and full of excellent detail, but they failed to fill the space.

Filling a space, though, is not merely a matter of projecting a performance into the auditorium. The on-stage space has to be filled too, sometimes by a single actor. In Mark Antony's speech 'O pardon me thou bleeding piece of earth,' he is alone on stage with Julius Caesar's freshly murdered body and, on first thoughts, nothing might seem more natural than for him to look down at it all the time he is talking. On television, he could, because the camera could move in close and his face, concentrating on Caesar, could fill the screen. But on stage, however well placed he is and however low he is kneeling or crouching (to avoid angling his head too sharply as he looks downwards) it is going to be impossible for him to focus his gaze on the body for twenty-two lines of blank verse without losing all contact with the audience. The stage has to be filled, not necessarily by moving about but by angling glances in different directions. This problem was exactly the same in

[1] Quoted in *The Player*, Lillian and Helen Ross. Simon and Schuster. For full details of books and articles quoted in the text see Appendix II, page 178.

the Elizabethan theatre and Shakespeare's script provides plenty of pretexts for looking away from the bleeding corpse. 'Woe to the hands that shed this costly blood' is one invitation for a glance in the direction that Brutus and the others have gone; and the prophecy that 'Domestic fury and fierce civil strife – Shall cumber all the parts of Italy' enables the actor's eye to travel all over the stage and all over the auditorium.

Different plays and different situations offer any number of different kinds of pretext for the eye to travel, but somehow the stage always has to be filled. Of course the ideal position for an actor is upstage, with characters on either side of him so that he can always be seen in full face and his eyes can linger momentarily out front as they move from one of his on-stage listeners to another, and linger longer while he is going through the equally important business of listening to them. The most difficult position for an actor is when he is alone on stage with one other character who is upstage of him. He then has to find reasons for looking away from him, both when he is speaking and when he is listening. Even in carrying on a conversation with another character who is level with him, an actor will, probably without thinking about it, find a justification for letting his eyes roam in a wide arc between his interlocutor and another point of focus – maybe a door or window on the other side of the stage, maybe a prop in his hand, held to the favourable side, maybe an imaginary point in the middle distance.

Consciously or unconsciously, the actor has to adapt to the audience, as to the space on-stage and off-stage which divides him from it. No two performances are ever exactly the same, and one of the variables that condition them is audience reaction, which influences the timing, among other things. In comedy it is not just a matter of giving the audience time to laugh: you also have to sense with each new audience how hard the points need to be hit. Audiences are less audible in serious plays and therefore harder to gauge, but each cough indicates (and foments) restlessness; not that you really need any sound at all to gauge how they are reacting. A good actor is always aware of audience temperature and, within limits, of how to control it.

Technique is not merely a matter of mechanics. An actor uses technique in stimulating and controlling his imagination and his feelings, as well as in using his voice and his body and adapting to the theatre and the audience. People often talk about 'the Method', which is derived more or less directly from Stanislavski's 'system', as if it were an alternative to technique. On the contrary, it is itself a technique for achieving a deep identification with the character and his circumstances. The good actor achieves this anyway when he is working at his best. It is only bad actors who come out of character and show that they are making efforts to obtain particular effects. All the efforts that are being made should seem to be coming from the character.

Once an actor has settled down into his identification with a part, his imagination will be concentrated on the circumstances surrounding the character at that moment and the power of his concentration will make them real for us. In order to react to them, he will not need to use his willpower at all: if the circumstances are real for him, the reaction will be automatic, the emotion spontaneous. If the character is in debt, for instance, and being pressured by his creditors, he only has to believe in the pressures for his reactions to become apparent. Only a bad director will say 'I want you to look more worried'; a good director will remind him that he may have to sell his car to raise the four hundred pounds he needs by this time next week.

If the character is angry or jealous or in love, the actor should never use his technique to simulate the emotion directly but to enter into the situation that gives rise to it. The kind of question that he needs to ask himself (or that the director needs to ask him) is not 'What are you feeling?' but 'What is happening?' Any deliberate manœuvring of face muscles to achieve a particular kind of expression can only produce phoney results. A large part of acting consists in re-acting and basically reactions are not voluntary.

If, in its articulation, the reaction needs to be controlled by the will-power, it is more likely to be in banking down the emotional fire than in stoking it up. The farewell scene, for instance, between Masha and Vershinin in *Three Sisters*, is most effective if the characters are trying *not* to give way to their emotions. When Stanislavski was playing Vershinin he tried to delay the moment of clasping Masha in his arms as long as possible, first not looking at her, then looking, and trying not to show emotion. Lee Strasberg,[1] who saw the performance, says 'I remember literally holding on to the seat. The simple reality of that goodbye, of the two people holding on as if they wouldn't let go, of both literally clinging to each other. . . .' Masha was trying not to weep. (The best way to weep on stage is to try not to.)

Where an actor may find himself in trouble is where he has to go through a series of actions that imply a pitch of feeling that he may reach at some performances and not others. Christopher Plummer had this problem as Henry II in Anouilh's *Becket* at the Aldwych when he had to knock a table over and leap about with a rage he did not always feel.

If it were possible to give a good performance just by will-ing your body to go through a certain series of actions and your voice through a series of sounds, the art of acting would consist in playing the voice and body expressively, like a musical instrument. The score of sounds and movements would need to be worked out as subtly and creatively as possible: you would be a composer in rehearsal and an auto-maton in performance. But the body is not a machine and, as an actor, you cannot be a technician without also being an artist. The technique is partly a matter of keeping the imagi-nation at work all the time, and keeping it in control.

Obviously the imaginative process and the physical process

[1] *Strasberg at the Actors' Studio*, ed. Robert H. Hethmon. Cape.

are interdependent. One move across the rehearsal room floor takes you much further than you can get by working in your flat and one reaction from the actor who is playing the scene with you takes you further still. The more interaction there is, the easier it is to identify with the characters and the situation. The actor only learns what the situation is from the words the playwright has written but for the audience those words must appear to be the result of the situation, not the cause of it.[1]

You also start to learn something in rehearsal – though you go on learning in performance – about what the other actors need from you. Brecht, who had very long rehearsal periods, used to take time to make his actors exchange roles so that each got to know exactly what the others needed from him. The more actors co-operate, the more creative the co-operation becomes. There is no clear line where stage business stops and improvisation begins and the more inventive actors are, the more interaction there is between them – interaction which cannot be charted in detail by the author's stage directions or the director's blocking. But it is up to the director to keep all this in check both during rehearsal and after the show has opened, by watching to see how much extra business has crept in and how much of it is good.[2]

While a lot of time in rehearsal is bound to be devoted to solving technical problems quite consciously, many of them are left to solve themselves while the actors, consciously absorbed with lines and relationships, simultaneously find out how to take advantage of the immense variety of choices which confronts them at every instant. Each gesture, each

[1] Kierkegaard has described very well what a great actress does to a script. 'Not only does she take the author's words correctly off his lips but she gives them back to him in such a way in the accompanying sound of her playfulness and the self-awareness of her genius, that she seems to say in addition "Let me see you copy that".' (*Crisis in the Life of an Actress*. Collins.)

[2] London productions, in particular musicals, suffer when a visiting American director goes back to the States after the first night, leaving the production in the hands of a Stage Manager who is not competent to direct.

inflection, each pause, each change of tempo could be played in dozens of different ways, and there is not time to make conscious decisions about all these points. If the actor's instincts are working well, and if his technique is good, his muscles will respond automatically to the flow of feeling that the situation produces and he will exteriorize what is going on inside him without puzzling about how to translate this emotion into that gesture.

The best technician is the actor who makes the best use of his talent and personality. Technique is only a means. Talent and personality are the beginning and the performance in front of a catalysing audience is the end. Like a dancer, the actor needs to be intimately aware of the advantages and the limitations of his own physique. He is only at his best when he makes use of both.

To some extent the basic physical equipment is pliable. The vocal training Sir Laurence Olivier did in preparation for playing Othello increased the depth of his voice by six tones. Robert Stephens trained at a gymnasium to build up his physique before playing Atahuelpa in *The Royal Hunt of the Sun* and Robert Brustein[1] was right to take Kim Stanley to task for failing to diet herself into a better shape to play Masha in the Actors' Studio production of *Three Sisters*.

It is not so easy to change your natural rhythms and patterns in speech and movement, but you need to be aware of them, and of how to go against them. The actors who cannot prevent their own personality from spilling all over their characters are very limited; a good actor can usually filter off what is inapposite for a particular character in a particular situation. And this filtering will be achieved partly through adjustments to other performances in rehearsal.

It is their capacity for this kind of adjustment that distinguishes comedy actors from comedians who cannot act. Even comedy actors like Maggie Smith, Kenneth Williams, Roy Kinnear and Sheila Hancock can filter off a great deal,

[1] Robert Brustein, *Seasons of Discontent*. Cape.

although there is something quite distinctive in their basic personalities which disposes an audience towards laughter. Maggie Smith has now improved her technique so much through her experience at the National Theatre that she has complete control over the elements in her personality that make it easy for her to be funny. Kenneth Williams's career has moved in the opposite direction. In the Fifties, as the Dauphin in *St Joan* and as a gentleman's gentleman in Mervyn Peake's comedy *The Wit to Woo*, he proved himself to be a very good actor but latterly, limiting himself more or less to 'Carry On' films and International Cabaret compèring, he inclines more and more to self-parody, becoming more of a comedian, less of an actor. The comedian has relationships with the audience and with his material – a triangle of relationships; the actor has a quadrilateral of relationships, for he also plays to the other actors. With comedians who cannot act, the failure in filtering is always connected with the failure to give anything to the other actors. Spike Milligan, for example, never stopped reminding us of himself as Ben Gunn in *Treasure Island*, as Mate in *The Bed-Sitting Room* or as Oblomov. In the play which started off as *Oblomov* and ended up as *Son of Oblomov*, he set out with the intention of acting – of creating a serious comic characterization and sticking to the scripted lines. But he started to feel insecure in rehearsals and took to ad-libbing in performance whenever he needed to reassure himself with a surefire gag. On the second night at the Lyric Hammersmith, a member of the audience sneezed and he said 'Bless you'. He was extremely funny and he was accoladed by a lot of the critics for parodying the whole convention of theatre, but by jumping in and out of character and in and out of the situation, he made things visibly difficult for the other actors. They had to adjust to him but he only adjusted to them in the way that comedians use stooges – by playing off them straight to the audience.

Nervousness is often a factor not only in this kind of over-eagerness to amuse but in the whole evolution of a comic personality. Dudley Moore has talked[1] about compensating for boyhood feelings of inferiority, which were due to his smallness, by developing the one thing he was quite sure he had – the ability to make other boys laugh. Kenneth Williams has also talked[1] about a nervousness which gets covered over in performance. But the surface effervescence has its sources in the pressure. Maggie Smith probably suffers from a similar nervousness. Though the surface is composed and the manner highly authoritative, it may be partly the faint suggestion of a tension underlying the composure which makes her so funny. She has a quality very similar to something in Judy Holliday which George Cukor described well when he said 'You had the feeling that she'd never spoken aloud before and you'd better catch it at that moment and you'd never hear it again.'[2] Myra's line 'This haddock is disgusting' in *Hay Fever* is not intrinsically memorable, but pointed as it was in Maggie Smith's flattest tones, it made it sound as though no haddock in history had ever been quite so upsetting.

Given a good technique, an actor's range is more likely to be limited by his temperament than by his physique. The better his technique, the wider his range, but few actors are protean enough to make you forget their own personality altogether as they slide into a character. Sir Alec Guinness, though, can do this. After seeing him play a dozen different parts, you still have very little idea about his own psychological make-up and you could probably sit opposite him in a railway carriage without recognizing him.

Of course it is hard for an actor to be objective about the limits of his range. Eric Porter has a very wide range but he went beyond it when, to reward him for his long and faithful services in *The Forsyte Saga*, the BBC offered him the choice of any part he wanted to play on television and he chose Cyrano de Bergerac. He had no difficulty with Cyrano's

[1] In a television interview.
[2] In an interview in *Double Exposure*. Delacorte Press.

stoicism but failed completely with his panache. He was quite convincing whenever he was being passive, contained, self-sacrificing, and he made the most of his death scene, but he lacks the verve and the aggressiveness to play a braggart like Cyrano who can back his boasts with sword thrusts. In the duels, he was just going through motions and in the scene where Cyrano interrupts the performance in the theatre, it was never credible for an instant that everyone else in the audience would have felt scared. Eric Porter has a highly developed technique, and it helped, but not enough.

At the National Theatre it was very interesting to see both Sir Michael Redgrave and Sir Laurence Olivier, who took over from him, playing the same part in the same production of *The Master Builder*. Good though they both were, temperamentally neither had quite the formidable range the part demands. The Master Builder is a self-made super-man, an artisan who rises so high that he loses sight of his own size and defies God. Redgrave was at his best in the scene about talking to God from the church tower, but he was never coarse or insensitive enough in his relationships with his fellow men or crude enough in his bluster about rejecting the title 'architect'. Olivier made Solness far more of a petty bourgeois and he was more convincingly selfish in his exploitation of Kaia, the secretary who loves him, and Ragnar, his assistant. He also extracted some unexpected comedy from his verbal sparring with Hilde Wangel, especially when Maggie Smith was playing the part. For ninety per cent of the play, his emphasis on the worldly, materialist side of Solness did no harm, but finally it was impossible to believe this man would have cared so much about his relationship with God.

I do not mean to suggest that an actor's emotional and psychological make-up is a constant. On the contrary, few people discover more than a small part of their own personality and an actor has more chances than most of exploring it. In fact he is only working at his best when he is exploring, whether taxing his resources to push into the unknown or passively staying open to the possibility of seeing something new. It might be a part or a director or an improvisation or another actor that suddenly produces a response in him which gives him a glimpse of something in himself he had never noticed before – a new kind of anger perhaps or a new tenderness. Usually it will be associated with a tone of voice that strikes him as unfamiliar. He may not even know what brought it there. And this process of self-discovery can go on indefinitely. Peter Ustinov has had more than twenty-five years' experience in a huge variety of parts but he said[1] that filming with Maggie Smith had made him find new things in himself.

This new experience for Ustinov resulted from having to adapt his performance to Maggie Smith's, and technique is always involved in the adaptations an actor has to make, whether to other actors, to the medium, the script, the style, the set, the costumes, the lighting, the props or the director. He also has to adapt to his own feelings, for there is a point beyond which he cannot control them. He may have had a serious quarrel with his wife which he cannot altogether put out of his mind during the performance: it will add bite to any similar scene he may have in the play but he must use all his self-control to keep himself from varying his performance too much. Or he may be suffering from a stomach upset or a headache bad enough to interfere with his concentration.

Quite apart from emotional or physical disturbances of this sort, one of his main problems is to repeat the performance night after night, giving himself sufficient scope for variation to keep it fresh and let it grow, but not so much scope that he is liable to throw the other actors off course. There is no general agreement – and it would be hard to formulate principles on which agreement could be reached – about the extent of the variations that are admissible. How can you measure variations? And even if you could, the answer would have to depend on circumstances – the style of

[1] In a talk at the National Film Theatre, 25th February 1968.

the production, how well the actors knew each other, how badly the other actors are likely to be affected.

To give two examples:

(1) At one performance in the middle of the run of a recent production at the Yvonne Arnaud Theatre, the actor playing the lead so altered his attack, his bearing, his timing and his whole manner that all the rehearsed tensions went out of his interactions with the rest of the cast, to be replaced by the visible tension of their anxiety about what he was going to do next. When the director rushed backstage to his dressing-room he said 'Yes, I started feeling it differently. It's better, isn't it?'

(2) Kenneth Tynan, who was the Player King in Alec Guinness's *Hamlet*, describes[1] a performance in which Rosencrantz spoke the line 'My Lord, you must tell us where the body is and go with us to the King' more brusquely than usual. Hamlet, who was at the other side of the stage, strode right across to him with a glassy smile and slapped the surprised actor hard across the ear. Afterwards in the wings, he rushed up to apologize. 'I'm sorry, but you were so *insolent* I felt I had to.'

Obviously the conduct of the actor at Guildford is indefensible but I think variations like Sir Alec's can be justifiable. Ideally, as Boris Zhakava put it, the actor responds to an expected stimulus as spontaneously and truthfully as to an unexpected stimulus. Spontaneity implies freedom, and in order to respond spontaneously to a line you are expecting, you have to allow yourself the freedom to depart from your normal reaction (or the normal reaction of the character you are playing) if a line strikes you differently, for whatever reason. Unless you allow yourself that freedom, you are playing within a strait-jacket of rehearsed reactions and the performance is no longer alive.

Meyerhold said 'The two main conditions of the actor's work are improvisation and the power of self-restraint. The

[1] Kenneth Tynan, *Alec Guinness*. Rockliff.

more complex the combination of these qualities, the greater the actor.' The extent to which an actor can improvise in performance is limited, but any variation in what happens around him, even if it is only a variation of the tone in which another actor addresses him, poses the question 'What am I going to do now?' and if he does what he has always done before, he may be acting untruthfully. The better an actor is, the more he will be liable to vary in performance and the more he will need technique, partly to control his inventiveness and partly to retain all the best things that he has discovered in rehearsals and in previous performances, without letting them go stale.

What I have been trying to do in this chapter has been

(1) to provide a rough sketch-map of the area in which technique operates, and

(2) to show that you cannot talk about it in the abstract because in practice it is always a matter of adapting something to something else.

2 · PERSONALITY, STYLE AND EMOTION

In our theatre – and in films and television even more – actors are constantly being thrown back on their own personalities, playing 'straight', using technique to present characters of the same physical and temperamental 'type' as they are themselves. But there have been, and there still are, styles of acting in which personality has a much smaller role to play.

In the Japanese Noh Theatre, which continues today in the same tradition that was established in the fourteenth century, the demands on the actors are very specific, the speech stylized, the individuality of the performers checked down by masks and ritualized movements. The dance element is important but it does not depend on anything like the big movements which the word 'dance' suggests to us. A movement may consist of nothing more than the slight lifting of one of the actor's kite-like sleeves. The main movement is in the voice. The sounds range from simple cooing legato bird-cries to complex monodic chants which are sometimes like plainsong and sometimes have jumps and wriggles in each vocal line. The actors are trained from childhood within family groups and they learn to reproduce the sounds and movements that their teacher makes with such detailed precision that personality barely enters into the performance.

Like the Noh actor, the classical Greek tragedian was not so much an entertainer as a celebrant at a public religious ceremony. He too was masked and he too depended less on personality than on a rather specialized technique. Aristotle defined acting as 'the right management of the voice to express the various emotions'. It is possible that the verse-speaking conventions made heavy demands on the voice; it is obvious that the vast arenas did, though amplifying devices may have been built into the masks. The actor's movements, though restricted by his costume, had to be larger than lifesize and the cothurnus, which lifted him well above his normal height, must have contributed to the depersonalizing effect. It is not surprising that no Greek actor made the same kind of mark on history as Roscius did – though he is said to have introduced masks to Rome in order to cover up his squint.

Modern acting started with the Elizabethans and there are plenty of clues in Hamlet's advice to the players about the virtues and vices of the contemporary style. His complaints about comedians who speak more than is set down for them may have been directed partly at William Kemp, who seems to have imitated the *commedia dell' arte* style of ad-libbing. But Burbage seems already to have practised a technique which today would have got him labelled as a Method actor, refusing to come out of character in his dressing-room. If Richard Flecknoe is to be believed – and he was writing forty-five years after Burbage's death[1] – he was

> a delightful Proteus, so wholly transforming himself into his part, and putting off himself with his clothes, as he never (not so much as in the 'tiring house) assum'd himself again until the play was done.

In the three centuries that have passed, styles have varied enormously and techniques have varied with them, but the actor never needed to have as many techniques at his command as he needs today. He needs to be at home working inside a proscenium, out on an apron stage or in-the-round and he must be able to adapt to the very different requirements of television, films, radio and recording. He should be able to work for traditionalist directors and experimenters, for the Brecht-oriented directors who have grown up out of the Royal Court, for Method-oriented Americans, for directors who still work equably in the same way as they did in the cosy days of Rattigan and for the television directors who concentrate on the cameras and give no notes to the actors except on angles and positions. He must be able to play Shakespeare and Hugh and Margaret Williams, Coward and Brecht, Farquhar and Feydeau, Shaw and Charles Wood. And he may often have to film or televise during the day, play on the stage in the evening and do a recording over the week-end.

In the eighteenth century, Shakespeare was rewritten in much the same style – and no doubt acted in much the same style – as if he were an eighteenth-century playwright. And in the Dark Ages of the nineteenth century, the play, the production and the supporting company were all liable to get sacrificed on the blood-stained altar of the actor-manager's

[1] Richard Flecknoe, *The Acting of Richard Burbage,* quoted in *The Elizabethan Stage.* O.U.P.

exorbitant ego. In the dim gas lighting, the main trick was
to get as far down towards the footlights as you could without
getting into the leading actor's way, and it was useless trying
to react subtly – only big movements could be seen. Today,
watching an actor's movements helps us to listen to what he is
saying and how he is inflecting – try sitting in an upper circle
with your eyes closed – but then he was much more dependent
on dominating the audience by sheer vocal force. Electricity
and the more enlightened actor-managers like William Poel
and Harley Granville-Barker all did a lot towards emancipat-
ing the actor.

Different periods imply different styles and different techniques: Sarah Bernhardt's acting can hardly be discussed in
the same terms as Marlon Brando's, and it is all too easy to
use words like 'truthfulness' and 'reality' as if they gave us
the exact location of a single goal at which all acting should
aim. Each generation of actors has thought itself more realistic than its predecessors and it is true, as John Mason Brown
has said, that 'Burbage would have thought Betterton too
mild, that Betterton would have missed strength in Garrick,
that Garrick would have been disappointed in Kean, Kean
in Irving, Irving in Gielgud, and Booth in Barrymore.'

From Bernhardt's point of view, there was no lack of truthfulness in her performances. She believed devoutly that it
was the actor's duty to 'forget himself and divest himself of
his proper attributes in order to attain those of the part . . .
Hamlet's frenzy will make the spectators shudder if he really
believes he is Hamlet.'[1] Naïvely enough, she regarded her
own art as realistic. 'The public,' she wrote, 'will not tolerate
any glossing over of reality.' From our point of view, her
public was extremely tolerant of thick coats of glossy romantic
emulsion paint, and there was only a small minority of dissi-
dent voices like Shaw's, who found her 'entirely inhuman and
incredible'.

Her audience, of course, wanted to shudder – to be startled

[1] Sarah Bernhardt, *The Art of the Theatre*. Bles.

by the emotional pyrotechnics of full-throated declamation and violent posturing. She was still working in the tradition of Kean, who considered it a tribute to his playing when spectators and fellow-actors fainted at his Sir Giles Over-reach. None of our Hamlets, from Gielgud to Nicol Williamson, have wound themselves up into a frenzy. Her whole style and approach were vastly different from ours; and it is quite possible that in fifty years from now, style will again have changed so much that audiences will watch films of our acting with the same bewilderment we feel in watching Bernhardt's. 'How on earth could they have raved about that?'[1]

Not that an actor's approach to his work was ever determined entirely by what contemporary audiences wanted. Garrick and Mrs Siddons acted together a great deal, playing in the same style for the same audience, but they could not have been more different in their basic approach to the art of acting. Garrick boasted that he could 'speak to a post with the same feelings and expression as to the loveliest Juliet under heaven' and Diderot described his virtuoso trick of going through a wide emotional gamut just to show off.

> Garrick will put his head between two folding doors, and in the course of five or six seconds his expression will change successively from wild delight to temperate pleasure, from this to tranquility, from tranquility to surprise, from surprise to blank astonishment, from that to fright, from fright to horror, from horror to despair, and thence will go up again to the point from which he started.[2]

Garrick would happily tell jokes in the intervals of a tragedy, while Mrs Siddons would get so involved in her part that often she would still be weeping when she arrived home. When she was playing Constance in *King John*, she would

[1] The fact that her effectiveness depended largely on her voice may partly explain why she comes out so badly on film.
[2] *The Paradox of Acting* (1773), translated by W. H. Pollock. Chatto.

never allow her dressing-room door to be closed all through the play. 'The spirit of the whole drama took possession of my mind and frame by my attention being incessantly riveted to the passing scenes.'[1] And while she was playing in Otway's *Venice Preserved*, she wrote 'Belvidera was hardly acting last night; I felt every word as if I were the real person and not the representative.'

You often hear actors talking as if technique were the alternative to 'really feeling it'. It is perfectly true that some actors, like Garrick, can switch the indications of emotion on and off very rapidly, while others, like Burbage or Mrs Siddons or Marlon Brando, prefer to be very slow at getting into character or coming out of character. This is not to say that they are using technique any less than an actor who is capable of whispering a joke to an extra just before launching into one of Hamlet's soliloquies. But obviously actors differ in the extent to which they are involved in the emotions that they are playing, and ever since Diderot's *Le Paradoxe sur le Comédien*, there have been incessant controversies about how much they ought to feel.

Writing perhaps with Garrick too much to the fore in his mind, Diderot argues that the ideal actor has no sensibility, his talent depending not on feeling but 'on rendering so exactly the outward signs of feeling that you fall into the trap'. G. H. Lewes, George Eliot's husband and one of the best nineteenth-century drama critics, made a much more open-minded attempt to answer the question of how far the actor feels the emotions he expresses.[2] He tells the story of how, in one performance, Talma got so carried away 'by the truth and beauty' of the lady playing opposite him that she had to calm him by whispering through clenched teeth 'Take care, Talma, you are moved'. And he quotes a self-indictment of Molé's, reproaching himself for losing control in identifying too completely with the part.

[1] *Actors on Acting*, Toby Cole and Helen Krich Chinoy. Crown.
[2] G. H. Lewes, *On Actors and the Art of Acting*.

I was not satisfied with myself tonight; I allowed myself to be carried away and did not remain master of myself. I felt the situation too strongly. I was the character himself, no longer the actor who played the part. I had become as real as if I were in my own home.

Lewes concludes that in performance the actor should be

in a state of emotional excitement sufficiently strong to furnish him with the elements of expression but not strong enough to prevent his modulating the one and arranging the other according to a preconceived standard.

Coquelin, who created the role of Cyrano de Bergerac, made some highly articulate pronouncements about acting. Paraphrasing a statement of Daudet's about the writer, he said that the actor must have two selves – the player and the instrument. The first self works on the second until it is transfigured, 'until from himself he has made his work of art', but it is the first self, the one which sees, that must remain master.

Whether you become frenzied to madness or suffer the pains of death, it must always be under the watchful eye of your ever-impassive first self and under fixed and prescribed bounds.[1]

Salvini, an actor Stanislavski greatly admired, later attacked Coquelin, objecting that as a theorist he was laying too much stress on detachment and that as a practitioner he did not feel enough on the stage to give the impression of being quite alive.[2] Not that Salvini himself was a thorough-going emotionalist.

An actor lives, weeps and laughs on the stage, and while weeping or laughing, he observes his laughter and tears.

[1] *Actors on Acting.*
[2] Tommaso Salvini, 'Some Views on Acting' (article in *Theatre Workshop*).

And it is in this dualism, in this equilibrium between life and acting, that art finds its true expression.

William Archer wrote a whole book on the question – *Masks or Faces? A Study in the Psychology of Acting*. After circulating a questionnaire to all the leading actors of the day, he was able to list the names of all those who had shed 'real tears' on the stage. He decides that emotion and detachment should be 'kneaded together' and in a chapter called 'The Brownies of the Brain' he concludes that 'the paradox of acting resolves itself into a paradox of dual consciousness'. But in substance he adds very little to the passage he quotes from Fanny Kemble describing her own state of mind on the stage.

The curious part of acting to me, is the sort of double process which the mind carries on at once, the combined operation of one's faculties, so to speak, in diametrically opposite directions; for instance, in the very last scene of Mrs Beverley, while I was half dead with crying in the midst of the *real* grief, created by an entirely unreal cause, I perceived that my tears were falling like rain all over my silk dress, and spoiling it; and I calculated and measured most accurately the space that my father would require to fall in, and moved myself and my train accordingly in the midst of the anguish I was to feign, and absolutely did endure. It is this watchful faculty (perfectly prosaic and commonplace in nature), which never deserts me while I am uttering all that exquisite passionate poetry in Juliet's balcony scene, while I feel as if my soul was on my lips and my colour comes and goes with the intensity of the sentiment I am expressing: which prevents me from falling over my train, from setting fire to myself with the lamps placed close to me, from leaning upon my canvas balcony when I seem to throw myself all but over it.

But the debate still rages, with the emotionalists citing

and over-simplifying Stanislavski and the anti-emotionalists citing and over-simplifying Brecht. Brecht was not against emotion on stage: he was against empathy, except at a certain stage of rehearsal. Stanislavski went through a phase of talking about 'the complete submergence of the actor into the role' but he soon came to realize that this was incompatible with self-control. In *An Actor Prepares*, he makes the director Tortsov urge his students to weep at home or in the rehearsal room so that they can rid themselves of all the excesses of sentiment which would get in the way of presenting the emotion clearly to an audience. 'Remembered emotion, not literal emotion,' was Vakhtangov's summing-up.

Ultimately the question of how much the actor feels is only important in so far as it is relevant to the question of how good his performance is. But it is relevant. The actor who feels nothing will fake and faking leads to cliché. What Stanislavski said about this was substantially the same as what Lewes had already said in 1875:

Within the limits which are assigned by nature to every artist, the success of the personation will depend upon the vividness of the actor's sympathy, and the honest reliance on the truth of his own individual expression, in preference to the conventional expressions which may be accepted on the stage. This is the great actor, the creative artist. The conventional artist is one who either because he does not feel the vivid sympathy, or cannot express what he feels, or has not sufficient energy or self-reliance to trust to his own expressions, cannot be the part, but tries to act it, and then is necessarily driven to adopt those conventional means of expression with which the traditions of the stage abound. Instead of allowing a strong feeling to express itself through its natural signs, he seizes upon the conventional signs, either because in truth there is no strong feeling moving him, or because he is not artist enough to give it genuine expression; his lips will curl, his brow wrinkle, his eyes be thrown up, his forehead be slapped, or he will grimace, rant and 'take the stage', in the style which has become traditional, but which was perhaps never seen off the stage; and thus he runs through the gamut of sounds and signs which bear as remote an affinity to any real expressions as the pantomimic conventions of ballet-dancers.

Although we underplay much more today, it would be easy to collect similar samples of clichés from the ones in use on both the stage and the screen. Every night on television you can watch performances which are bad because the actors rely too much on the fact that they have been cast according to type rather than thinking out their performances – except in terms of the effect they want to make; and they do half the audience's work for it. 'I am a loud-mouthed bully who is a coward at heart and I want them to see through me.' 'I am a well-meaning dupe and I want them to feel a mixture of pity and contempt.'

Lewes's point is still valid. My only quarrel is with his division of actors into two distinct classes – creative actors who have the plasticity to express feelings through their vivid sympathy with the characters and conventional actors who are using a different technique, collecting effects like postage stamps to stick over the gap inside, where nothing very much is going on. The trouble with pigeon-holing actors like this is that it makes you forget that the majority of actors have a foot in each pigeon-hole. There are quite a lot of bad actors who are consistently 'imitative', but there are few actors, if any, who are creative at every moment of every performance every night, thinking out each speech, each reaction freshly, never using tricks, never coasting, never imitating anyone else, never even imitating themselves, never repeating an effect because it went well last night. There are some who sink comparatively seldom on to the level of stale, second-hand effects; there are many who rise only seldom above that level.

So rather than say that there are two kinds of actor, it would be better to say that there are two kinds of acting involving two kinds of technique and that most actors oscillate between the two during each performance.

---

3 · THE INSIDE AND OUTSIDE OF A CHARACTERIZATION

For all the evils of pigeon-holing, it is hard to get away from it altogether because the labels on the conventional pigeon-holes are basic to the very limited vocabulary we have. What we need to do is go on using the names on the labels, but without pushing actors into the pigeon-holes.

The six most common ways of dividing actors into two categories are

(1) 'Method' and technical
(2) Creative and imitative
(3) Straight and character
(4) Actors who find the role in themselves and actors who find themselves in the role
(5) Internal and external
(6) Actors who start from the inside and work outwards and actors who start on the outside and work inwards.

The first pair of categories is almost meaningless and we have already discussed (2). The third, when it is applied to actors (as opposed to parts or performances) is very dangerous. It was all very well in the days of the old-fashioned repertory companies when the 'leading man' and the 'leading lady' always played 'straight', week after week, and 'character actors' were employed to play the 'character parts'. But *Spotlight*, the illustrated casting directory in which nearly every actor in the country advertises twice a year, still divides both men and women into four classes – leading and younger leading; character; younger character; juvenile and juvenile character. Actors have nerve-racking discussions with agents, wives and friends about whether they'd have got more work if their photographs had gone into a different section. Are they 'younger' or 'juvenile'? Should they classify themselves on the basis of how good-looking they are or how protean? At one time, if you were not good-looking, you had to be fairly protean to survive in the profession, but things are different now. In any case, many good-looking actors, like John Neville and Paul Daneman, who usually play 'leading men' consider themselves better – I think rightly – at character work. Even Gielgud has done most of his best work in character parts.

Early in Laurence Olivier's career Clare Eames said to him: 'Don't tell me there's such a thing as a straight part. There isn't a part in the world that isn't a character part.' When he came round to this point of view it affected the whole of his subsequent development, and perhaps it would be a good thing for English acting if the third pair of categories were abandoned altogether.

The fourth is much more useful and it was interesting to hear Dame Edith Evans and Dame Sybil Thorndike talking in such very similar terms in their television interviews for the *Great Acting* series[1] about what they had found inside themselves.

MICHAEL ELLIOTT: How is it that you have managed to play so many different kinds of part?
DAME EDITH: I don't really know, except that I seemed to have an awful lot of people inside me. Do you know what I

[1] Reprinted in *Great Acting*, B.B.C. Publications.

mean? If I understand them I feel terribly like them when I'm doing them.

MICHAEL ELLIOTT: I think it was Herbert Farjeon who said about you, 'She has the great power to become what she thinks she is.'

DAME EDITH: Yes, yes, by thinking you turn into the person, if you think it strongly enough. It's quite odd sometimes, you know. You are it, for quite a bit, and then you're not. It's what I call bridges.

MICHAEL ELLIOTT: During rehearsals?

DAME EDITH: Yes, you can't find the bridge to be that woman. Maybe it's a little fault in the writing, maybe it's a fault in you. Then I have to work very hard to make the woman that I can know join up to the one that I can't know. . . .

MICHAEL MACOWAN: You've never been stuck with one kind of person, have you?

DAME SYBIL: No, I haven't. I'm saying this, and it isn't mock-modest; but I've never been a wildly attractive person, which was, really, to my joy, because I was able to do all sorts of things that an attractive girl wouldn't. I loved acting and playing people. It was also a means of finding out about people, and making the audience like them. You say, 'Come on, this is what this old bitch is like, now you can understand her.'

MICHAEL MACOWAN: It is a particular feature of your work, that you can play the most horrible people doing terrible things but, somehow, it never is unpleasant; when you do it, one understands them.

DAME SYBIL: Now that goes deep into what I believe, because I believe that within us we've got the germ of every other sort of person. If I can play a terrible part which I can find somewhere inside me, then, but for the grace of God, I might have been that person. I can never forget that after playing the *Medea*, I felt as though I'd been in a bath.

You can get rid of all sorts of embryo awfulness and throw them off. All the foul tempers, wanting to knock Lewis's block off, wanting to spank the children, I got rid of them all. The family used to say I was angelic after playing the *Medea*.

There is a curious sidelight on the same feeling in Ionesco's Preface to *Les Possédés* adapted from Dostoevski by Akakia Viala and Nicolas Bataille.[1] It was Bataille who staged Ionesco's first play *La Cantatrice Chauve* at the Théâtre de Poche and he then invited Ionesco to play Stepan Trofimovich in *Les Possédés*.

I had learned that each of us is all the others, that my solitude had not been real and that the actor can, better than anyone else, understand human beings by understanding himself. In learning to act, I have also, in a certain sense, learned to admit that the others are oneself, that you yourself are the others, and that all lonelinesses become identified.

The danger of the fifth pair of categories is that it produces a confusion between (2) and (6), though it ought to be obvious that an actor who starts on the outside is not necessarily going to remain on the outside and give a superficial performance. It depends how far inwards he works, and how successfully. In a good performance, a very great deal is going on both on the inside and on the outside, and it does not matter which develops out of which. What matters is when they meet up and how they interconnect.

Sir Laurence Olivier starts on the outside. He confessed to Kenneth Tynan[2] that his characterization of Richard III at the Old Vic grew out of a determination to be different from Donald Wolfit, who had played the part very success-

---

[1] Martin Esslin has quoted this in *The Theatre of the Absurd*. Eyre & Spottiswoode.

[2] In an interview in *Great Acting*.

fully eighteen months beforehand. He then started planning what kind of voice to use.

> First of all I had heard imitations of old actors imitating Henry Irving; and so I did, right away, an imitation of these old actors imitating Henry Irving's voice – that's why I took a rather narrow kind of vocal address. Then I thought about looks. And I thought about the Big Bad Wolf, and I thought about Jed Harris, a director under whom I'd suffered *in extremis* in New York. The physiognomy of Disney's original Big Bad Wolf was said to have been founded upon Jed Harris – hence the nose, which originally was very much bigger than it was finally in the film. And so, with one or two extraneous externals, I began to build up a character, a characterization. I'm afraid I do work mostly from the outside in. I usually collect a lot of details, a lot of characteristics, and find a creature swimming about somewhere in the middle of them . . .

The 'I'm afraid' is symptomatic of a guilt so many actors feel about starting on the outside, not because of Stanislavski, who knew it was often necessary, but because of the way his teachings have been distorted by his disciples. And if you ask whether Olivier would have done better to start work on Richard III from the inside, the only answer is that this performance could not have been achieved in any other way.

The other external factor that influenced his conception of the part was Hitler. He first played Richard at the Old Vic in the last year of the war, and he did not make the film of the play until 1955, but when Richard barks out orders with his voice tightening into a hysterical shriek, it still makes one think of Hitler. It is not a flawless performance by any means but Olivier certainly succeeded in integrating all these elements he picked up from outside.

The relationship with the audience (or the camera) is much more subtly contrived than the relationships with the other protagonists. In the early soliloquies he presents a

Richard who is surprisingly self-satisfied – never neurotic about his personal appearance and essentially a man of action who gets tetchy when he has to wait. The monologues are flung straight into the camera, not just as a humorous choric commentary but as signposts to what is going on in his mind, as he amuses himself with an almost camp relish for his ironically measured vowel-sounds and the consonants that he taps out so fiercely with his tongue. The violence of certain gestures in this time of leisure prepares us for what is to come and the viciousness of his sarcasm prefigures his viciousness in action when he has power.

Olivier is at his best when the volcano after prolonged rumblings erupts into physical action. After Buckingham's suave oratory has gulled the citizens into speaking up for Richard as King, he swings triumphantly down into the courtyard on a bellrope, and thrusting his twisted hand out, like a weapon, for Buckingham to kiss, he abruptly lowers it so that the astonished orator, who expected thanks, has to stoop even lower. Sitting on the throne and briefing Tyrrell about the murder of the young princes, he snatches a cushion from behind him and nearly suffocates the murderer in showing him how to do it. At the end of the film his death throes are superbly effective, the small bent body still flailing about half-consciously with blind feeble thrusts at enemies who are no longer there.

At points like this, the outside and the inside of the characterization correspond perfectly, each feeding the other, but there are also points where they do not, where the voice hardens mechanically as Olivier forces vocal climaxes unnecessarily early. Altogether, the interrelationships with other characters only work when they flare up into spectacular visual effects. But Richard is essentially a con man. He works his way to the top by getting people to trust him. Buckingham believes that at least Richard will play fair with him, if not with the others, and the others are convinced of his whole-hearted sincerity. Olivier himself has said that if he had to define acting in one sentence, he would call it 'the art of persuasion. The actor persuades himself, first, and through himself, the audience'. But he also has to persuade the other characters, and to be taken in by this Richard, Buckingham and the others would have had to be very stupid indeed.

To take a specific example of the opposite way of working – starting on the inside – we have Stanislavski's account of his own characterization of Dr Stockmann in Ibsen's *An Enemy of the People*.

> When I was working on the part of Stockmann, it was Stockmann's love and his craving for truth that interested me most in the play and in my part. It was by intuition, instinctively, that I came to understand the inner nature of Ibsen's character, with all his peculiarities, his childishness, his short-sightedness, which told me of Stockmann's inner blindness to human vices, of his comradely attitude to his wife, and children, of his cheerfulness and vivacity. I fell under the spell of Stockmann's personality, which made all who came in contact with him better and purer men and revealed the better sides of their natures in his presence.
>
> It was my intuition that suggested to me Stockmann's outward appearance: it grew naturally out of the inner man. Stockmann's and Stanislavski's body and soul fused organically with one another. The moment I thought of Dr Stockmann's thoughts and worries, his shortsightedness appeared by itself; I saw the forward stoop of his body and his hurried gait. The first and second fingers were thrust forward by themselves as though with the intention of ramming my feelings, words and thoughts into the very soul of the man I was talking to.[1]

This is probably as good an example as any of characterization in which the actor arrived at the outward appearance

[1] *Stanislavski on the Art of the Stage.* Faber.

he was to adopt through an intuition about the inner man. But it is always an over-simplification to say that an actor 'started on the inside' or 'started on the outside'. He may start off with a more definite idea of one or the other but he nearly always starts simultaneously on both the inside and outside, and goes on working from the outside inwards at the same time as he works from the inside outwards. Stanislavski had a very useful intuition about Stockmann's 'inner image' but he also worked into his characterization a number of physical details which he picked up from memories and observations of friends, though without realizing what he was doing until much later.

> A few years passed and I still played Stockmann, and little by little I found accidentally the sources of many of the elements of the inner and outer images. For instance, in Berlin, I met a learned man whom I had often met before in a sanatorium near Vienna, and I recognized that I had taken the fingers of Stockmann's hand from him . . . Meeting a famous musical critic I recognized in him my manner of stamping in one place in the role of Stockmann.[1]

Nor is it just a matter of working simultaneously from the outside inwards and from the inside outwards: the right kind of progress in one direction encourages progress in the other, and very soon it becomes unimportant which bits of characterization started where.

What is very important, though, is the first moment of getting a clear visual impression of the character, whether in the mind's eye or in the dressing-room mirror. Sometimes this moment comes very late. Working on *The Prime of Miss Jean Brodie*, Vanessa Redgrave found that there were two crucial moments in her visualization of Jean Brodie's character. The first only occurred a few days before the final dress rehearsal and the play had already opened before the second.

[1] Stanislavski, *My Life in Art*. Bles.

How I eventually found her was finding out what she wanted to be like. She longs to be like Garbo, Pavlova, Thorndike. And so we made her dress in colours and materials and designs that were, to a certain extent, successful realizations of her dreams. It wasn't until I was in those damned clothes on the stage, four days from going out on tour, that I suddenly knew that what was vital was that Brodie is and looks like a dried-up spinster; that what makes her ironic and pathetic is that she is not, *not* for any single minute of her breathing life, what she wants to be. So then we found the plainness – you know, simple, neat clothes – and just added an Eastern bangle or Eastern belt from her voyages. We got to Torquay on the tour and I still had a completely different wig, a Sybil-Thorndike-in-*Saint-Joan* wig. But we had a smooth wig hanging by, which had been rejected. I suddenly thought one night, I'm going to put the other wig on. And I thought of Anna Pavlova making up in her dressing-room, and so I did my hair trying to be as near to the classical ballerina line as I could. Thinking of that, I suddenly found I *was* Brodie; that was when I got nearest to Brodie, because that was all that Brodie could want to be like.[1]

Every actor has experiences more or less like this with make-up and costume. Suddenly there is something about the figure in the mirror that you no longer recognize. It has acquired an independence from you. It has its own way of speaking and moving which you can no longer control quite in the way you did in all the previous rehearsals but you no longer need to. You feel safe. The character has acquired a backbone, strong but supple, and whatever variations get introduced subsequently, something basic has come right, which you know you can count on to go on giving you support.

One of the most revealing passages in all Stanislavski's

[1] Vanessa Redgrave in a television interview, reprinted in *The Listener*.

work is the story in *Building a Character* of how Kostya hits on a make-up through playing around with a greenish removing cream. Something begins to take shape in his imagination and he becomes more deliberate in what he does, smearing it into his wig, his moustache and his beard. He rearranges his clothes and starts walking with his toes turned in, which makes him look shorter. Looking into the mirror again, he has the impression of being someone else and when one of the teachers comes to the dressing-room, he finds himself speaking in a hoarse voice and with unusual self-confidence. His laugh becomes a shrill snigger. One leg, twisted more than the other, pitches his body over to the right and limping on to the stage, he finds that for the first time in his life, he is being extremely rude to Tortsov.

This is one of the most exciting sensations in all acting – the feeling of being in control and out of control at the same time, liberated from yourself and from all your normal inhibitions and anxieties. You are circumscribed only by the character. Something has been born for which you are both responsible and not responsible.

///

4 · IS STANISLAVSKI OUT OF DATE?

Stanislavski's achievement was massive and magnificent. He was the first great actor-director-teacher to make a thorough exploration of technique and to leave detailed charts of his voyages. Many of his ideas and formulations will go on being valuable as long as the art of acting survives and we have absorbed so many elements of Stanislavski into our theatrical bloodstream that we no longer know when we are under his influence.

But in many ways he belongs more to the nineteenth century than to the twentieth. He was born in 1863 and he grew up into a theatre which was riddled with rusting productions of rusting melodramas. When he and Nemirovich-Danchenko founded the Moscow Art Theatre, settings and productions were customarily standardized. There was a sofa stage right, a table and two chairs stage left and a clear space above the prompter's box. These three areas were used in rotation. Canvas doors shivered when they were opened, stars who were greeted with applause bowed to acknowledge it and the orchestra was conspicuous all through the action, even in a straight play. Stanislavski did a great deal towards changing all this and giving his theatre what it needed – a far more deeply thought out and thorough-going naturalism. Not that he should be dismissed as an apostle of naturalism: he also championed symbolism, even if he chose Maeterlinck as his representative of it. But this is the theatre in which his ideas evolved.

He was also a religious man, whose approach to art, as to life, was basically a religious one. Liberal in outlook, he believed in human goodness and the possibility of progress. Even when he was giving notes to actors, he spoke with a high seriousness almost worthy of Matthew Arnold.

> The greater your goodwill towards men and the purer your thoughts, the greater the number of beautiful qualities that you will discern in your neighbour. The lower the level of your feelings and thoughts, the more evil will you see around you, for you have to make an effort to see what is good, while you need no effort at all to see evil.[1]

For Stanislavski, acting was very much a matter of faith. 'Nine tenths of the labour of an actor,' he wrote, 'nine tenths of everything lies in beginning to live and feel the role spiritually.' These are not merely perfunctory bows in the direction of piety and spirituality. He profoundly believed

[1] *Stanislavski on the Art of the Stage.*

that the theatrical experience was in the nature of a communion in which both actor and audience rose above the baser parts of their nature, so that the actor could 'transmit the great raptures of the human soul' and the audience could 'enter into the soul of the actor through the eyes,'

> every spectator recognizing in him the better parts of himself, suffering and weeping, rejoicing and laughing, and taking part with all his heart in the life of the character in the play.[1]

This is why he advised every actor to arrive in the theatre two hours before the curtain so as to have time to 'make-up and dress his soul for the life of the human spirit in the part'.

In this context, the stress on 'believing' takes on an almost religious significance. The actor has to believe in everything that is happening on stage around him, developing a 'child-like naïveté' which is essential to the faith which will transform painted scenery and contrived props into reality.

Above all, he must believe in what he does himself and Stanislavski was rigorous in scrutinizing his own work as an actor for any untruthfulness. He describes in *My Life in Art* how he found himself going into unnatural poses that he could not believe in.

> I took a certain pose on the stage. I did not believe in it physically. Here and there I weakened the strain. It was better. Now I changed the pose somewhat. Ah! I understood. When one stretches himself in order to reach something, this pose is the result of such stretching. And my whole body and after it my soul, began to believe that I was stretching towards an object which I needed very much.

There are still devotees of Stanislavski who say that everything that needs to be known about acting can be found in his work and that in order to translate it into twentieth-

[1] *Stanislavski on the Art of the Stage.*

century terms, all you need to do is substitute the words 'mind' or 'psyche' for the words 'spirit' or 'soul'. But Stanislavski believed in a very simple correlation between physical actions and 'inner psychological actions'. Every physical action must have an inner action which gives rise to it; every inner action must have a physical action which expresses its psychic nature. And, believing in the soul, he believed that there would be complete harmony between all the inner actions going on inside a character.

Of course there are characters who can be played in these terms without over-simplification. Dr Stockmann is one of them and it is revealing that as an actor Stanislavski felt more at home in this part than in any other. But Stockmann is a very simple soul who never experiences any inner conflicts. He is a wholly good man who always wants to do what is right and he is naïvely unsuspecting about his fellow-citizens, who do not. Less public-spirited than he is, they experience no difficulty in turning their backs on the truth when their private interests are threatened by it and it does not occur to Stockmann that they will penalize him for speaking out about the poison in the public water supply. But even when he realizes that the path of duty will lead to suffering for his wife and children, as well as for himself, he follows it without involving himself in any inner conflict.

But in Chekhov, even the simplest characters are more complicated than this, and although Stanislavski loved Chekhov and launched him as a playwright, he did not altogether understand him. After seeing Stanislavski's performance as Trigorin in *The Seagull*, Chekhov said 'Your acting is excellent, only you're not playing my character. I didn't write that'. And it took Stanislavski over a year to realize that Trigorin should not be handsome and elegant, even after Chekhov had told him that he ought to wear torn shoes and check trousers.

Altogether Chekhov is far subtler than Stanislavski, far

more capable of handling tendencies that pull in different directions and much further in advance of contemporary Russian theatre practice. His reaction to Stanislavski's production of *The Seagull* was to ask him to end the play with Act Three; he walked out of the first company meeting of *Three Sisters*; and after *The Cherry Orchard* he said 'Stanislavski has ruined the play for me'.

It was hard to tell how much of Stanislavski's production survived in the impressive but over-serious staging of the play that the Moscow Art Theatre brought to Sadler's Wells in 1951 but it is easy to see from what Stanislavski has written about *The Seagull*, both in his autobiography and in his production notes, that his approach would be much too heavy-handed for *The Cherry Orchard*. He even misses the irony in Chekhov's presentation of Konstantin Treplev's views about theatre.

> Listen to the essence of his art and you find that it is a complete grammar for the actor of today . . . How talented is this Treplev with the soul of Chekhov and a true comprehension of art.[1]

His elaborations of Chekhov's stage directions sentimentalize them.

> *Chekhov:* Masha (dances a few waltz steps noiselessly). 'The chief thing, mother is not to see him.'
> *Stanislavski:* Masha sighs again, waltzes to the window, stops beside it, looks out into the darkness, and stealthily wipes the few tears that roll down her cheeks. A pause (the music goes on). Pauline stops making the bed and looks thoughtfully at her daughter. (She has evidently remembered her own love affair with Dorn.)[2]

Where Chekhov suggests, Stanislavski emphasizes. At one point he has Konstantin beating his breast, at another, where

[1] Stanislavski, *My Life in Art.*
[2] *The Seagull produced by Stanislavski.* Dobson.

Chekhov wants him to embrace Dorn impulsively, Stanislavski has him kissing him nervously and sitting down to bury his face in a handkerchief. And where Chekhov wants Konstantin to cross out what he has written, Stanislavski makes him tear the page out and throw it away. He even alters Chekhov's text, crossing out the words 'I'm a seagull. No, that's not it. I'm an actress. Yes!' when they occur at the beginning of Nina's famous speech in Act Four. (She says the first two phrases again in the middle of the speech.)

Sound-effects are important in Chekhov, but instead of suggesting a mood or an atmosphere by using just a few, Stanislavski writes a whole tone poem into his production script at each point. Chekhov wanted *The Seagull* to start with the sounds of workmen hammering and coughing. Stanislavski adds the distant sounds of a drunkard's song, the distant howling of a dog, the croaking of frogs, the crake of a landrail, the slow tolling of a distant church-bell, the faint rumbling of thunder and a workman humming a tune.

But for all the laborious detail of his realism, the effects produced on the stage could not stand up to comparison with reality. Preparing for his production of Tolstoy's *The Powers of Darkness*, he went to live in Tula for two weeks to visit the nearest villages with his designer and his wardrobe mistress. They brought back drawings, furniture, costumes and two peasants – an old man and an old woman. When the actress playing Matriona was ill, the old peasant woman stood in for her and proved herself to be so effective that Tolstoy's son asked whether she could take over the part. Stanislavski agreed and the actress agreed to stand down. But the old woman was so good that only one actress in the company (Butova, who played Anisya) could hold her own. The others all seemed so unreal that Stanislavski gave his actress back her part and put the old woman into the crowd. There she made the others look phoney, so he hid her in the back row, but even there, one note of her weeping made the exclamations of the others sound false. Unwilling to lose her, he interpolated a pause in which she was to cross the stage droning a song and calling someone in the distance.

> The sound of the old and weak voice was possessed of such breadth and gave the spirit of the Russian village with such veracity that it was impossible for any one of us to appear on the stage after her exit.[1]

In the end they recorded her voice and used it as a background to the action.

Stanislavski's experience in trying to play Act Two of *A Month in the Country* in the park of the palace at Kiev also casts some doubt on the 'truthfulness' of their realism.

> We began our improvised performance with a great deal of aplomb. My turn also came, and now Knipper-Chekhova and I, as we are supposed to do in the play, walked along a long alley-path, repeating our text, and then sat down on a bench, according to our usual *mise-en-scène*, and – I stopped, because I could not stop my false and theatrical pose. All that I had done seemed untrue to nature, to reality. And it had been said of us that we had developed simplicity to a point of naturalism! How far we are from simple human speech, how conventional we saw to be what we had become used to do on the stage, considering our scenic truth to be real truth.[1]

There's no accurate way of measuring our realism against Stanislavski's but our actors are used to working in the open air in films and television; and television has been even more effective than films in encouraging underplaying, partly because performances brought right into the home need to be smaller – there's no question of 'filling a space' here. And of course acting styles on the screen affect acting styles on the stage. Irving would have been a very different actor if television had been invented a hundred years earlier, and so would Stanislavski. Since it reflects his own practice as an

[1] Stanislavski, *My Life in Art*.

actor and as a director, his writing is inevitably prone to the same faults.

The basic fault is over-simplification about the relationship between the motive and the action. He not only over-simplified consistently, he attributed the success of his Moscow Art Theatre productions to the reduction of all the actor's drives and objectives to a single drive (which he called) *through-going action* and to a single objective, which he called the *super-objective*.

> I work a great deal, and it is my considered opinion that there are only two things that count in the final analysis: the super-objective and the through-going action – that is the main thing in the art of acting . . . Why did audiences like us? Because we understood our super-objective. And when we did not understand it we got nothing right.[1]

In *An Actor Prepares*, Tortsov teaches his students how to break up a play – and a role – into 'units' and 'objectives'. In each unit, the actor has to know what his objective is, what his will-power is reaching for, and the concept of 'through-going action' suggests that if all the objectives were represented by arrows, they should all be pointing in the same direction. Tortsov draws a diagram on the blackboard.

$$\longrightarrow \;\;\rightarrow\;\;\rightarrow\;\;\rightarrow\;\;\rightarrow\!\boxed{\text{THE SUPER-OBJECTIVE}}$$

The Through Line of Action
'All the minor lines are headed towards the same goal and fuse into one main current,' he explained. 'Let us take the case, however, of an actor who has not established his ultimate purpose, whose part is made up of smaller lines leading in varying directions. Then we have:

[1] *Stanislavski on the Art of the Stage.*

'If all the minor objectives in a part are aimed in different directions it is, of course, impossible to form a solid, unbroken line. Consequently the action is fragmentary, unco-ordinated, unrelated to any whole. No matter how excellent each part may be in itself, it has no place in the play on that basis.

'Let me give you another case. We have agreed, have we not, that the main line of action and the main theme are organically part of the play and they cannot be disregarded without detriment to the play itself. But suppose we were to introduce an extraneous theme or put what you might call a tendency into the play. The other elements will remain the same but they will be turned aside, by this new addition. It can be expressed this way:

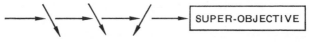

Tendency

'A play with that kind of deformed, broken backbone cannot live.'[1]

According to Tortsov the drive of a whole play can be summed up in a single sentence – always a sentence expressing a wish. The super-objective of *Le Malade Imaginaire* is 'I wish to be thought sick'; that of Goldoni's *La Locandiera* 'I wish to do my courting on the sly.'

This approach is valid only for uncomplicated characters like Stockmann, whose motives are consistent, and conscious, and whose actions co-ordinate logically with them. But already in 1888, Strindberg was complaining (in the preface to *Miss Julie*) about characterization which assumed that people were homogeneous.

Because they are modern characters, living in a period of transition more hysterically hurried than its immediate

[1] Stanislavski, *An Actor Prepares*. Bles.

predecessor at least, I have made my figures vacillating, out of joint, torn between the old and the new . . . My souls (or characters) are conglomerates, made up of past and present stages of civilization, scraps of humanity, torn-off pieces of Sunday clothing turned into rags – all patched together as is the human soul itself.

Since then, in Strindberg's own later work, in Pirandello, Brecht, Beckett, Ionesco, Pinter and Genet, and in dozens of other writers, the substance of character has become far more volatile, the concept of the integrity of the personality more and more discredited. The arrows have to go in a dozen different directions.

Today there can be far less emphasis on will-power in either the character or the actor. We can no longer believe, that, as Vakhtangov put it, 'the fundamental thing which an actor must learn is to wish, to wish by order and to wish whatever is given to the character'. We know we do not know what we want and we know we do not know what our motives are. We no longer tell ourselves we know where we are going and we are not sure we would want to go there if we did. The fragmentation in our novels and paintings and films reflects a lack of faith in discernible pattern. Artists tend to assume that if there is a pattern to be found at all, it is such an inextricably complicated one that we can only hope to find part of it and that we are more likely to do that accidentally than by setting out to look for it. Working on a play like the *Marat-Sade* by Peter Weiss, it is essential to break it up into units, but the only way to put the pieces together is in a mosaic, not thinking in a through line. If Liv Ullmann in Bergman's film *Persona* or Anna Karina in Jean-Luc Godard's *Pierrot le Fou* had tried to think in terms of a super-objective, they would have found the parts unplayable.

The point is often made that there is no such thing as Stanislavski's 'theory of acting'. As he went on working in the theatre, he changed his mind on a great many points and the later books sometimes contradict the earlier. This is exactly as it should be; but he was also liable to contradict himself inside the covers of a single book. Here are two passages from his most influential book of all, *An Actor Prepares*, both on the crucial point of how far an actor should be immersed in the part.

> Always act in your own person, as an artist. You can never get away from yourself. The moment you lose yourself on the stage marks the departure from truly living your part and the beginning of exaggerated false acting . . . Always use your own feelings . . . always play yourself. (page 177)
> Your head will swim from the sudden and complete fusion of your life with your part . . . You will be incapable of distinguishing between yourself and the person you are portraying . . . Then . . . truth and faith will lead you into the region of the subconscious and hand you over to the power of nature. (page 295)

Together the two formulations make it very unclear how much identification Stanislavski wanted, and the constantly reiterated appeals to truth and faith only confuse the issue.

Every good actor knows the feeling of simultaneously being himself and someone else who only partly overlaps with himself, but on this point the actress Geraldine Page is much more lucid than Stanislavski.

> Sometimes the character comes out in ways which surprise me . . . If I do something, and a bell rings somewhere in me, and it feels right, I have a tendency to repeat what I did and to find other pieces that fit in with it. It's like a jig-saw puzzle. After the opening of a play, a lot more little pieces come in late . . . When you take the character over and use the character, you wreck the fabric of the play, but you can be in control of the character without taking the character over. When the character uses you, that's when

you're really cooking. You know you're in complete control, yet you get the feeling that you didn't do it. You have this beautiful feeling that you can't ruin it.[1]

//

5 · *BRECHT AND HIS INFLUENCE*

Many of Brecht's criticisms of Stanislavski had been made already by Stanislavski's own pupils. Vakhtangov thought it was essential for an actor to separate himself from his role sufficiently to show his attitude to it and to history as a whole and he condemned Stanislavski for taking pleasure in the fact that audiences came to the Moscow Art Theatre's production of *Three Sisters* as if they had been invited to the Prozorovs' house. Brecht, whose chief aim in the theatre was to stimulate his audiences into thinking critically about the structure of society, was bound to be hostile to anything that put the audience into a mood of acceptance.

What he (Stanislavski) cared about was naturalness, and as a result everything in his theatre seemed far too natural for anyone to pause and go into it thoroughly. You don't normally examine your own home or your own feeding habits, do you?[2]

This was the main object of alienation – to make the audience pause and go into it thoroughly – whatever *it* was. What Brecht liked about Chinese acting was that it made individual movements stand out in a clear relief: whether he was representing a cloud or a human character, the Chinese actor would not try to merge his own identity fully into it.

[1] *The Player*, Lillian and Helen Ross. Simon & Schuster.
[2] *Brecht on Theatre*. Ed. John Willett. Methuen. This is the source of the other Brecht quotations unless a different source is specified.

In his essay *Alienation Effects in Chinese Acting*, Brecht describes the difference between an actor reproducing the symptoms of emotion without feeling it and an actor producing an alienation effect. You can fake anger by letting your voice rise, holding your breath and tightening your neck muscles so that the blood shoots up in the head.

> In such a case of course the effect does not occur. But it does occur if the actor at a particular point unexpectedly shows a completely white face, which he has produced mechanically by holding his face in his hands with some white make-up on them. If the actor at the same time displays an apparently composed character, then his terror at this point (as a result of this message, or that discovery) will give rise to an alienation effect.

In an article in a Berlin paper in February 1929, Brecht had described how the young Helene Weigel had adapted this method of producing the effect in her performance as the servant in *Oedipus Rex*.

> She announced the death of her mistress by calling out her 'Dead, dead' in a wholly unemotional and penetrating voice, her 'Jocasta has died' without any sorrow but so firmly and definitely that the bare fact of her mistress's death carried more weight at that precise moment than could have been generated by any grief of her own. She did not abandon her voice to horror, but perhaps her face, for she used white make-up to show the impact which a death makes on all who are present at it. Her announcement that the suicide had collapsed as if before a beater was made up less of pity for this collapse than of pride in the beater's achievement, so that it became plain to even the most emotionally punch-drunk spectator that here a decision had been carried out which called for his acquiescence.

This was only a few months after Brecht married Weigel

and a year before he started publishing his theories about epic theatre. Already she was producing an alienation effect and recoiling hard against the emotional style of acting. Brecht's emphasis in the article, like hers in the performance, was on 'the bare facts'. The appeal Brechtian acting has today is closely connected with this belief that a simple statement of the facts can be more effective, more telling emotionally, than a display of emotion. But whereas the death of Jocasta calls for acquiescence in the audience, Brecht was more often interested in provoking from them a query – 'Was this necessary? Did it have to happen this way?' So it was up to the actor to play in such a way that nothing would seem inevitable. At all costs, the audience must be prevented from saying to themselves 'That was only to be expected from a character like that'.

As a pointer to the kind of acting he wanted, Brecht was fond of instancing a bystander's description of a street accident to a crowd who did not see it. He plays both parts: the driver behind the wheel and the old man who was knocked down. In either part, he does the minimum necessary to make the crowd visualize how it happened, and he is submitting the driver to their judgement. He makes it clear that both men could have moved quite differently: nothing was pre-determined. He cares about getting the details right, knowing that it may depend on his evidence whether the injured party receives damages. But he never tries to transform himself into the people he is imitating, never tries to hide the limitations in his knowledge about the two men. At any moment he could be interrupted in his performance and he interrupts himself to check whether he is making any mistakes.

How far did Brecht want the actor to follow this model? He wanted to avoid the mysterious transformation by which an actor leaves the dressing-room and a king walks on to the stage. The Brechtian actor will get rid of all suggestions of magic or trance; and like the witness of the accident, he will make it clear that what he is acting out was not inevitable.

> When he appears on the stage, besides what he actually is doing he will at all essential points discover, specify, imply what he is not doing; that is to say he will act in such a way that the alternative emerges as clearly as possible, that his acting allows the other possibilities to be inferred and only represents one out of the possible variants ...

In order to achieve this result, Brecht advises the actor to memorize his own reactions on reading the script for the first time. If his character's behaviour sometimes strikes him as odd or quirky, or if he is surprised by some of the events which overtake him in the action, he must preserve his own reactions so that he can make use of them in the performance, presenting not just a character and a set of actions, but an attitude towards them.

On this point, Brecht's position was quite irreconcilable with Stanislavski's. Stanislavski believed that any such division in the actor's consciousness would prevent him from creating a character which is clear in its purpose. Once the actor started thinking about the character or the action critically and trying to communicate his criticism to the audience, he would destroy the single-minded concentration on his superobjective which was necessary if the arrows were all to go in a straight line. For Stanislavski, the actor is only truthful so long as he believes in this polarity and pieces all the elements in his performance together in accordance with it. For Brecht, it is essential for the actor to take account of the inconsistencies in his character.

> The coherence of the character is in fact shown by the way in which its individual qualities contradict one another.

So far, so good. Brecht's interest in the contradictions is

far more modern than Stanislavski's insistence on single-mindedness, and his approach is not based on a premiss of omniscience. But his viewpoint was not psychological; it was social and historical. The importance of any line of script, any moment of action, was not what it showed about the individual but what it showed about society at that moment in its history.

Just what difference does this make in practice? This becomes clear from two examples Brecht took himself.

(1) The New York Yiddish Theatre put on a play about an East Side boy who becomes a crooked lawyer. In one scene a young woman gets desperate when her leg, injured in a traffic accident, has started to heal and because her case has been bungled, she still hasn't received any compensation. Brecht complained that in playing the line 'It's started to heal up' as if her desperation were perfectly natural, the actress was unable to use the unnaturalness of the character's attitude 'to show the horror of a bloody epoch'.

(2) A hypothetical incident – a girl is leaving home and her mother, generous enough with advice, is packing very little food into her suitcase. How must the mother speak her line as she hands over the little bag – 'So I think that's enough' – for it to stand out as a historical statement? It can only be achieved if the alienation effect is produced. The actress must not make the line into a thing of her own. She must submit it to criticism, she must make it possible for us to understand its motivation and to protest.

When Brecht and Weigel founded the Berliner Ensemble in 1949, a distinctive style and technique of acting and production were evolved which were to have a huge influence on acting all over the world. The actor, like the playwright and like the director, approaches his material partly from a social-historical viewpoint and this affects not only the pointing of individual lines but the basic conception of a characterization.

Helene Weigel's characterization of the rich farmer's wife

in Strittmatter's play *Katzgraben* is an example. *Katzgraben* is a very bad verse play about conflicts between smallholders and local farmers in the German Democratic Republic. Brecht directed it himself in 1953 and there were some excellent performances, of which Weigel's was the best. When she was asked why she had given the rich farmer's wife hunched shoulders and a goitre, her reply was:

> That shows he married her for her money. And if I hadn't put money into his farm, he wouldn't put up with the way I boss everybody about. Without the money, I myself would never have dreamed of behaving like this, because I was religiously brought up to believe that the wife is subordinate to the husband.[1]

And Angelika Hurwicz, who achieved such extraordinary depth in *Mother Courage* as the dumb daughter Kattrin, started off by looking at the role in a very wide perspective.

> Working on this role, I learnt the difference between realism and naturalism. If I'd played the dumbness as the result of an injury done to the tongue (and Courage has a line in Scene 6: 'A soldier let her have it in the mouth when she was small') that means that if I'd rolled my tongue forward against my teeth when I was uttering sounds, the way you can see deaf-mutes doing it, my expression could very easily have become rather idiotic. It would have been quite wrong to give an impression of retarded development. What was important was to show that intelligent people, born to happiness, can be crippled by war. Precision in portraying an individual case had to be sacrificed for this general truth.[2]

It is not enough for a character to be interesting in itself and theatrically effective: it also has to be representative of something – a group, a social abuse, a set of social and economic

---

[1] Berliner Ensemble notes of a rehearsal discussion.
[2] Quoted in *Theaterarbeit*, a Berliner Ensemble publication.

circumstances. This might seem to mean that the characters become 'types', and some of the Berliner Ensemble characterizations of unsympathetic figures like employers and land-owners did fail in this way, but less often and less seriously than might have been expected. And in the best performances, like Weigel's and Hurwicz's in *Mother Courage*, the characterizations are highly individualized, at the same time as typifying the damage that war can do to the mind and the body.

Both actresses educe enormous sympathy for the characters they play. The fact that Brecht asked his actors to think critically and to avoid total immersion in the parts does not mean that Brechtian acting is unemotional. Weigel had to look at Mother Courage from outside to see her in her social and historical context and to see how stupid the woman is: she also got inside to find out what it felt like to be driven by Courage's needs and compulsions. The resultant performance is all the more moving because it is so well counterweighted.

Our sympathy for what the woman suffers is balanced by our disapproval of what she does. We like her vitality, her courage, her toughness, her shrewdness and her capacity for non-stop hard work. We dislike her stupidity, her refusal or inability to learn from experience and her meanness. We have to recognize that what costs her the lives of both her sons is a middle-class quality (love of business for business's sake) deeply embedded in a working-class habit of life. She is selling a belt to the sergeant while the recruiting officer makes off with her elder son Eilif; and later, when by selling her wagon to the camp whore she could have raised enough ransom money to save her second son's life, she haggles too long over the price and he is killed.

In each of these passages, the actress sharpens the writer's point. Her impatience with Dumb Kattrin, who tries to warn her that the recruiting officer is whetting Eilif's interest, focuses her almost sensual enjoyment of the act of selling, and it is only after she has snapped her purse shut that she realizes Eilif is no longer there. She has to sit down on the wagon shaft to recover. Then she flings her belts angrily into the wagon and forces herself to go on.

The death of the second son produces two superb moments in Weigel's performance. When she hears the salvo that kills him, her head goes back and her lips part in a silent scream, agonized to the limit of her endurance. Brecht thought she was probably drawing on an unconscious memory of a newspaper photograph of an Indian woman squatting by the corpse of her son during the shelling of Singapore. Weigel had seen the photograph but forgotten it. The second moment comes when the corpse is brought in. From sitting down, holding Kattrin's hand, Weigel gets up, her features fixed in an ice-hard determination not to give herself away. The lower lip is thrust forward. Holding her head stiffly and her hands clasped, she walks over to the corpse, shakes her head, walks back, sits down again with no change at all in the expression on her face. But the feeling is expressed perfectly by refusing it any outlet. It is as clear here as anywhere in the play that Mother Courage has got what it takes to survive, but it is clearer here than anywhere else how much it costs. It is an extremely moving piece of self-control on both Weigel's part and Courage's, but the actress is not completely immersed in the character and she is not drawing our pity but making a critical point. Our reaction is not: 'Poor woman! Look what she has to go through just to stay alive!' It is: 'Look what her actions have led her to and look how hard she is!'

Asked in an interview[1] how much she worked from observation, Weigel said

Often I observe something and know for sure, that's a point that I can use in a particular role. But mostly you don't know where the ideas come from. Observation and imagination often complement each other. That's what happened

---

[1] Quoted in *Theaterarbeit*.

in *Die Mutter*. The gentleness in Pelagea Wlassowa's gait and manner grew out of the idea of giving her a drooping left shoulder. For someone who grows that way isn't very pushing. Or Mother Courage's purse. That was an observed prop which you then exploit in the characterization. The way the purse clicks when you shut it gives you a whole range of possibilities – shutting it lightly and quickly or as in giving over the money at Kattrin's burial. Once – in the scene where Yvette arrives with the old Colonel – I built it up into a veritable aria of clicks. Observation also contributed to the variations in Courage's tone of voice: in Scene 9, for example – in the Fichtelgebirge in the grim cold when there's no business and nothing for it but to beg – the voice is dull, flabby; in spite of carrying on with the dialect, she gets more and more monotonous. That was worked out from a lot of things I've seen at various times – people in the street and so on.

The performance, like the play, is great because it absorbs such a huge and varied mass of human raw material, and then recreates it.

In reply to the question 'Why do you act?' Charles Laughton once said 'Because people don't know what they're like and I think I can show them'. Brecht was also interested in showing people what they were like, but only for the sake of changing them, and his belief in theatre as a means of promulgating change amounted to a faith. This, oddly, is where he resembles Stanislavski. The intensity of his belief gave him the power to produce a rehearsal atmosphere of complete dedication. Each prop, each pause, each inflection had to be got exactly right. More was at stake than an evening's entertainment for a paying audience. Every element in the production must contribute to telling the truth.

The careful documentation of rehearsal discussions is typical of the Berliner Ensemble, and, thanks to them, it is possible to reproduce what happened at one rehearsal of

Katzgraben. Brecht's productions could never have achieved the great precision they did without this kind of attention to detail.

STRITTMATTER: The small farmer should still be laughing at the big farmer's joke when he sees the money. His laughter breaks off abruptly.

BRECHT: And the paying of the debt must become an important historic event. Kleinschmidt has pulled his worn out wallet carefully and ceremoniously out of his pocket and now he sits down at the table expressly to be able to carry out the action.

(The actor Friedrich Gnass rehearses this.)

BRECHT: Gnass, it's not easy to handle bank notes with hands that are used to ploughing. Show that exactly.

STRITTMATTER: Blow on the bundle of notes to separate them and spit on your right thumb to help you count the money. No, don't lick your thumb. Kleinschmidt finds bank notes disgusting.

(This is rehearsed.)

BRECHT: Do that once again please but when Mittelländer's laugh breaks off, don't come in with your line straight away. Go on counting out the money, first, note by note, very slowly. Take your time.

(The scene is played like this but it takes several attempts before the actor Gnass dares to pause long enough to satisfy Brecht.

Then an assistant who's sitting in the back row making notes suggests that Kleinschmidt should pay out all the money he has in the wallet to make it clear that in order to pay his debts he's actually paying out everything he has left after buying the ox – the money he's earned from his double harvest.)

BRECHT: To make him appear honest? I don't know.

THE ASSISTANT: No of course not. Paying his debts is a political action. He wants to win the small farmer to his side. He doesn't mind paying for that.

BRECHT: Good, that's an important point. But he must keep two banknotes. On the stage, a little money is less than no money at all.

By talking of historic moments and political actions, the actors both alienate themselves from what they are doing and make it more significant. The incentive to accuracy is enormous.

In the detail of stage business, as in the reaction against the rhetorical over-emotional style of acting that was rife in the German theatre when Brecht started work, he pinned his faith in the bare facts. He did not want the audience to be overwhelmed or emotionally exhausted by the actors' displays of emotion. The audience was to be stimulated to pass judgement, just as the crowd in the street would form an opinion of whether the accident was the driver's fault or the pedestrian's. This does not mean that Brechtian acting should not provoke feelings in the audience. On the contrary, Brecht often criticized his actors in rehearsal for falling short in natural warmth, underplaying, showing too little temperament.

Like Stanislavski, Brecht was a moralist, but his ideas of right and wrong derived mainly from Marx. His sympathies were against the bosses and with the masses, so theatrically his influence has made acting less heroic and less romantic at the same time as producing a reaction against the Freudian approach. Of course, influences are never seen in their pure state, and the ripples that spread from the Berliner Ensemble have mixed with other currents in changing the tide of English theatrical fashion. When the London theatre still had not recovered from *Waiting for Godot* which had opened in August 1955, *Look Back in Anger* opened in May 1956 and the Berliner Ensemble brought over three of their productions in August. Heroes were never again going to be so heroic and the theatre was never again going to be so much a preserve of middle-class individualism.

Obviously it simplifies things to talk of pre-Brechtian and post-Brechtian acting, but it is not misleading. This is what Kenneth Tynan said to me in an interview in 1966 about some of Sir Laurence Olivier's performances at the National Theatre.

> I think Larry would have played Othello quite different-ly twenty years ago. This is an unromantic Othello – a wild animal, unheroic. This wouldn't have been possible in the pre-Brecht period. And his Brazen (in *The Recruiting Officer*) would have been much more like his Mr Puff (in *The Critic*), not the sleazy club bore that he is. I don't know whether his Master Builder would have been different.
>
> R.H. What about Tattle in *Love for Love*?
>
> K.T. That's different too. With his dirty lace and his pasty complexion, he's not doing it in the Nigel Playfair way at all.

And the performances of the stars themselves are partly governed by the extent to which the theatre is given over to the star system. Robert Shaw has complained[1] of stratifica-tion at Stratford-on-Avon in the 1950 season when the middle ranks were chosen for their usefulness to the stars and the stars all tended to listen to their own voices.

There has been a major change in the role of the small-part actor. In the ten years after the war, crowds were treated much more like choruses in an opera, manœuvred by the producer for picturesque groupings. But an anti-heroic production style pays much more heed to the ordinary facts in the life of the ordinary man. In recent Royal Shakespeare Company productions of the history plays, the soldiers came much more into the foreground – life-like men who panted and sweated and got tired and thirsty from lugging around realistic boxes of ammunition and dragging heavy-looking carts. Just as Brecht depended much more on objects in

[1] In *The Player*, Lillian and Helen Ross.

the foreground than on backcloths to create the atmosphere of a locale and made Mother Courage pluck a real chicken in an unrealistic set, the actor now needs to be much more precise and realistic in how he handles his props. Objects can be made to take on much more life than they traditionally have done.

Because there is less of a gulf between the star and the supporting actor, the supporting actor can very rapidly become a star. At Stratford-on-Avon it would not have been possible to cast a David Warner as Hamlet or an Ian Holm as Henry V before 1956. By his casting, Peter Hall was doing what Brecht had been doing for years in Berlin – downgrading the King socially, placing the emphasis on what he has in common with the masses, not on what differentiates him from them. By his voice, his stance, his gestures and the way he played with his scarf, David Warner underlined the common multiples between Hamlet and any student at any Redbrick university and he spoke the soliloquies more like a worried man than a noble hero. Nicol Williamson has since gone still further in this direction. Gielgud's Hamlet made the tragedy inevitable: David Warner seemed quite capable of behaving differently, less honourably, and the fact that he seemed to have more option made his death moving in quite a different way. Nicol Williamson's Hamlet had less freedom but because of his compulsiveness, not enough nobility. He was a powerful, snarling Hamlet, not very likeable until the second half of the play and more like a modern unemployed Birmingham factory worker than a prince. He put the emphasis on the melancholia and gave it the overtones of a class grievance.

As the hero becomes less noble, he becomes less spiritual. Crudely expressed, what we have had is a shift from Stanislavskian spirituality to Brechtian materialism. This ought not to imply a shift away from speaking the verse as verse but some reaction was no doubt to be expected from the tradition in which one actor would consciously copy another's cadences. In his book *Mask or Face*, Sir Michael Redgrave – and all credit to him for being honest about it – describes how in *Richard II* he followed Sir John Gielgud's 'phrasing and breathing' and his 'technical framework' (whatever he means by that).

Certainly we want to get away from copying and from the artificial glorification of sound at the expense of sense and it is good to hear actors like David Warner and Ian Holm working their way through soliloquies as if they are really trying to think things out as they go along. But Gielgud did that too and the reaction against him has gone too far. It ought to be possible to keep more of Shakespeare's rhythms without losing any of the new colloquial freshness and directness, simply by finding a rhythm in thinking which corresponds to the speech rhythm, but it is surprising how seldom actors bring this off.

The point about Shakespearian blank verse is that if the rhythm is not given its value, the images will not get theirs either. When Gielgud was directing Richard Burton in *Hamlet* he gave the cast good advice.

If one puts the commas and full stops in the right place and phrases the thing as it's written, and the players are not tempted, as I notice a lot of people were tending to do yesterday, to jump their bridges, it will all go better.

I want it to be swift, but if you give away the fact that you know what's coming next, it gives an effect of memorization or gabbling. You must try to empty your minds of the next phrase before it comes, and then place it accurately in the right position as it follows. Do you know what I mean? As in real life, one often doesn't know quite what one is going to say next; but at the same time in a poetic text one mustn't pause and make great holes in the play in order to appear natural – that one cannot do. Somehow it must be so carefully rehearsed that the thoughts are ready to come into your mind before the words so that you sew the speech behind your thought, so that it doesn't appear glib – then it will somehow seem to have a freshness.[1]

Gielgud has also made the point[2] that Shakespeare can write as flatly and naturalistically as he wants to. 'Pray you, undo this button.' And there are passages of prose dialogue in between the verse dialogue. The actor who flattens everything into prose is, apart from anything else, losing out on the chances of variation Shakespeare has provided him with.

It is very dangerous to swing too far away from the natural rhythms of the verse just in order to find something new. Even Paul Scofield was oddly erratic in his 1967 Macbeth. When I saw this at Stratford-on-Avon, early on in the run, he was so anxious to get away from the familiar *Macbeth* mould that he was breaking the verse up into idiosyncratic short cadences with innumerable brief pauses that had nothing to do with the sense. I saw the production again at the Aldwych on the last night of the run (10th April, 1968) and by then he had settled down to a far more legato performance, keeping his original broken rhythm only in one speech – 'Tomorrow and tomorrow and tomorrow'. Here it serves a very useful purpose, reflecting Macbeth's crack-up: he can no longer think smoothly. The fragmentation which was fatal for the whole performance was fine for the one speech. In the same way that in 1962 he had made King Lear much more of an angry old man and much less of a colossus detonating with justifiable indignation at being cheated of his rights, he made Macbeth much more like an ordinary soldier – tough, bearish, brave, easily led. It was less of a surprise than usual that he was unable to resist the persuasions of Vivien Merchant's coolly sexy Lady Macbeth or to cope with the situations that

---

[1] Quoted in Richard L. Sterne, *John Gielgud Directs Richard Burton in Hamlet.* Heinemann Educational Books.

[2] In *Stage Directions.* Heinemann Educational Books.

the various murders unleash. He never seemed stronger or better or in any way more heroic than Macduff or Banquo.

If the star is more like a supporting actor today, the supporting actor is more like a star, and has to reckon with being in focus more. An instance of how Brecht can affect the demands a director makes on 'supporting' actors is provided by William Gaskill's experience over the scene between the two murderers before they kill Clarence in *Richard III*.[1] At Stratford-on-Avon in 1961 Gaskill had two very good actors in the parts, Gordon Gostelow and Russell Hunter, but the scene never quite worked for him and he could never understand why. When he was rehearsing for his production of Brecht's *Caucasian Chalk Circle* at the Aldwych in 1962 he again had Gostelow and Hunter in his cast and he took the scene as the basis for an improvisation. What he then discovered was that they had played it at Stratford as a scene about a sadist and a coward who had come to murder the Duke; the actors had played the men's individual emotions, ignoring their social conditioning. But murder was much more common in Shakespeare's time – and in Richard III's – and the two men were professionals. Through Brecht, Gaskill discovered that for the scene to work, it was necessary both to show how habitual the act of killing was and to put the habit in a critical perspective. As in the play about the crooked lawyer, there can be a danger of the actor's sinking so uncritically into the character's situation that he misses the playwright's point.

Although it is obvious that the spread of Brecht's influence has done actors, playwrights, directors, casting directors, designers and even lighting designers far more good than harm, it is also true that certain plays suffer when approached in a Brechtian spirit. The Berliner Ensemble has always been rigorously selective in its repertoire and it badly damaged Synge's *Playboy of the Western World* by making it into a parable to prove that killing one's father was typical of the violence which Western civilization admired in its heroes. (A

---

[1] William Gaskill. Interview with the Editors of *Encore*.

ballad was introduced to drive the point home and the play was retitled *The Hero of the Western World*.) The Ensemble would never produce plays like Beckett's or Albee's, but the pupils, less discerning than the master, often introduce Brechtian stylistic tricks – which are essentially focusing devices – into plays where the focus ought to be on the personal and emotional foreground. This can produce insoluble problems for actors, who may be elbowed into playing a social sub-text which undermines the play that the playwright wrote.

Broadly speaking, the Brechtian approach tends to shift the focus away from personal relationships, and while it was high time for both the theatre and cinema to be pushed into spreading their nets wider, Brecht's misinterpretation of Ibsen's *Doll's House* is indicative of the kind of damage that can be done by forcing his approach into the wrong play.

> Ibsen had great intelligence and he was a sound playwright, but in a play like *The Doll's House*, what does he do? The husband is a banker, and he wants to see whether the wife has an equal right to be a banker. That is what she wants – to deal with accounts and financial affairs like her husband. But I don't think Ibsen knew very much about banking. And the play has no meaning for society today. To be a banker! Just the question of whether it's right for a woman to do the work of her husband . . . The real question is what Nora would do with her freedom if she had it.[1]

It is true that Nora gets into trouble because she raises money to pay for a holiday without telling Helmer, her husband, and forges her father's signature on the bond, but she is not so much concerned to prove her right to dabble in money matters or her aptitude for them as to preserve her life of carefree dependence on her fussy middle-class husband. Ibsen establishes her as emotionally immature in the first scene when we see her sucking macaroons and lying about them to

[1] R. H. 'A Last Interview with Brecht', *London Magazine*, November, 1956.

Helmer, who has forbidden them. As far as she knows, she is happy in the role of his little singing bird. But the key scene comes just before the end when she finds that she is not: for eight years she has not had a single serious conversation with him. Like her father, he has played with her but never tried to understand her, used her but never loved her as an equal. An actress who played the part according to Brecht's interpretation by making Nora ambitious for economic parity with Helmer, would be making her far too conscious far too soon. The desire for freedom comes only when she finds out that she has been deprived of it all this time and the play is about the deprivation, not about what she would do with her freedom if she had it. Certainly *The Doll's House* is making a social comment but the best way for the actress to make Ibsen's point is by gaining sympathy for Nora while she submits to Helmer's private oppression and then she will have still more sympathy when her consciousness suddenly jerks her into rebelling. Throughout Acts One and Two, she is passive with Helmer and her own active energy is harnessed almost entirely to covering up what she has done. She gets plenty of opportunities to be charming with Helmer, with Krogstad, her creditor, and with her children, but this charm, which seems to be her main feature, can be sloughed off like a snake's skin, once she gives up trying to cling on to her position in the household. The play is partly about her relationship with Helmer but still more about her relationship with herself.

On the whole, at this point in theatrical history, more is to be gained from Brecht than from Stanislavski, and Jean-Luc Godard has spectacularly shown how cinema can utilize the gains. But we cannot live by Brecht alone.

6 · CHARACTER

Of all the theatrical words which get used loosely, the one that most urgently needs re-definition is *character*. On the face of it the meaning is simple enough and quite unmistakable: the character is the person that the actor plays. He uses his own personality to present to the audience the personality of another person, which the playwright has imagined, and he selects, just as the playwright has, certain characteristics for greater emphasis. Every playwright has to create characters of one sort or another but Beckett and Pinter characterize in a very different way from Ibsen, just as novelists and film-makers today characterize by selecting and presenting characteristics in a very different way from their more naturalistic predecessors. In the cinema, directors and editors can tailor naturalistic acting performances into an end-product which vastly changes the appearance of the ingredients that went into it, but in the theatre we still suffer from old-fashioned overdoses of naturalism. It is time for some fresh thinking about 'character'.

Stanislavski's assumption that all the inner movements of the psyche and all the outward expressions of the personality would naturally harmonize was already too old-fashioned to cope with the discords of Chekhov and Strindberg. Brecht's insistence that the coherence of a character resides in the way his individual qualities contradict each other is much more modern, but the problem of how the actor should make the contradictions cohere is not entirely solved by the injunction that he should stand partly outside the character. Obviously, even if he is playing a character who acts inconsistently, he needs a basis on which he can interrelate his principal characteristics: he cannot present the audience with a bundle of scraps of human behaviour without himself understanding something about the relationship between them. But how much does he need to know? The answer can no longer be 'Everything'. And how is he going to cope with the areas where the playwright condemns him to remain ignorant?

It is only now that it is becoming obvious how stubbornly the nineteenth-century view of character has survived into the twentieth. With Shakespeare, literary criticism has moved far ahead of the nineteenth-century view of character, but the theatre has lagged behind, as if books like A. C. Bradley's *Shakespearean Tragedy* (1904) were still up to date. Bradley did nearly all his thinking in terms of character and he treated characters as if they were real people, analysing their personality-structure and trying to reconstruct their off-stage movements. The notes at the end of his lectures have headings like 'Where was Hamlet at the time of his father's death?' 'Did Emilia suspect Iago?' and 'When was the murder of Duncan first plotted?'

His approach is to be seen at its worst in his two lectures on *Othello*, which he sees as a 'tragedy of character'. 'Iago's plot,' he says, 'is Iago's character in action,' adding that the plot 'is built on his knowledge of Othello's character and could not otherwise have succeeded.' This kind of criticism must push the actor in the direction of psychological analysis – the action is made to hinge on Iago's insight into the way Othello's mind works. There are still critics who enjoy applying analytical psychology to Shakespeare's characters, but F. R. Leavis, who has been most influential in attacking this approach, makes the point that Shakespeare did not create people. He put words together. Obviously the characters' behaviour has to be convincing – they could not perform their dramatic function otherwise – but it is the dramatic function which is important, not the personality and not the scenes in the character's life which the writer did not write.

Usually the influence of a critic on an actor is indirect and difficult to prove or to analyse, but Dr Leavis had an even more direct influence on Olivier's Othello than Jan Kott had on the Brook-Scofield *King Lear*. Kenneth Tynan has described how Olivier came to the first read-through of the play and tossed his characterization out at the rest of the company 'like a hand grenade'. In the interview with Tynan, I questioned the wisdom of this, wondering whether the fact that Olivier had done so much work on the part before going into rehearsal might help to explain why his performance had stayed so isolated from the rest of the production.

K.T.: Yes, but he wasn't trying to dominate the others. He was trying to spur them on. It was a challenge for them if they dared to behave as extravagantly as he did, sitting with spectacles on at a table.

R.H.: But wouldn't it have been better if the performance had been worked out in collaboration with the other actors?

K.T.: Well, it was worked out in collaboration with the director and me. I got John Dexter to read Dr Leavis's essay on *Othello* and Dexter gave it to him.

The essay, which is a refutation of Bradley's account of the play, stresses how simple-minded Othello's behaviour is, how quickly he responds to Iago's insinuations about Desdemona, how egotistic he is and how self-dramatizing. 'The mind that undoes him is not Iago's but his own . . . Iago is subordinate and merely ancillary.' Critics have wasted a huge amount of ink and energy discussing whether the motives Iago himself puts forward for his own behaviour are his real motives. In the first scene he tells Roderigo that he hates Othello for passing him over when he appointed Cassio as lieutenant, fobbing Iago off with the job of ancient or ensign; in his soliloquy at the end of Act One he says it is thought abroad that Othello has been to bed with Emilia, and this suspicion is voiced again in the next scene when Iago says that he too loves Desdemona and wants to be 'even'd with him, wife for wife'. He also says he suspects Cassio of sleeping with Emilia. In Act Five there is the same tendency for Iago to give too many reasons for doing something the plot requires him to do: the writing is both perfunctory and over-scrupulous at the same time. After setting Roderigo on to killing Cassio, and inflaming his anger to the right murderous pitch, he stops to explain that he does not mind whether it is Cassio or Roderigo who gets killed. Roderigo is becoming tiresome because he is asking too many questions about the gold and jewels he has given Iago as gifts for Desdemona; Cassio is tiresome because he has a daily beauty in his life that makes Iago ugly. Besides he is dangerous, because Othello might find out from him that Iago's slanders are inventions.

Are these motivations valid or relevant? Or is Iago, as Othello says, a demi-devil (a human bastard with a devil for one parent) in which case his evil deeds would not need any explanation? Or does it matter? All that really matters is what Iago says and does on stage. To play the part, of course, the actor needs to feel that he knows a lot about Iago – what he looks like, whether he is twenty-eight ('I have looked upon the world for four times seven years') or older, how he moves, how he handles a sword, how much he changes between the soliloquies when he is just being himself and the scenes when he is putting on an act for the other characters. But he will learn far more of what he needs to know about Iago from studying the movement of the lines Shakespeare has written for him – how one thought leads to the next, the mixed feelings of superiority and inferiority, the mixed love and hate for Othello – than he will from asking Freudian questions about his motives or biographical questions about his off-stage life. His motives or his motivelessness are only relevant in so far as they affect what happens on stage.

In any case, as M. C. Bradbrook has pointed out in her excellent book, *Themes and Conventions of Elizabethan Tragedy*, motivations were more conventional than realistic and there were plays like Tourneur's *A Revenger's Tragedy* in which a very complicated plot centred on a very simple desire for revenge in the hero. This was not so much a realistic motive, capable of analysis, as a prerequisite of the action, a *donnée*. But Shakespeare and even Tourneur have to be reinterpreted by each period according to its own premisses and new productions of old plays are bound to be influenced by new plays, just as Beckett and Brecht both influenced Peter Brook's *King Lear*.

According to the Bradleyan view, character centred on a single overriding passion. Othello could be equated with jealousy, Macbeth with ambition, Lear with anger and Hamlet with revenge. This view must have dovetailed very nicely with the windy rhetorical displays of passion our tragedians indulged in around the turn of the century but today we are so used to seeing motivations as complicated and even contradictory, that there has to be altogether less stress on the individual's passion and will power. One of the reasons why Shakespearian heroes are less heroic today is that it is no longer possible to wish for anything, even for revenge, with the same passionate singleness of purpose – the same through-line of action leading towards the super-objective.

Today we no longer suffer so much from rhetorical acting, which overplays the passion, but some actors go about the task of preparing a character as if they were writing a nine-teenth-century naturalistic novel, treating the fiction as fact and working on the conscious or unconscious assumption that the more information they can collect about their character, the better their final performance will be. And some directors encourage them. The American actor Paul Mann, who is head of the actor training programme at Lincoln Centre, described to the *Tulane Drama Review* how he worked under Kazan's direction in Arthur Miller's *After the Fall*. He created a complete history of what happened to his character (the Father) before, during and after the action of the play. He made up specific stories about every character he had a relationship with. He told the girl playing his secretary how much he paid her. He drew up floor-plans of the house and the office.

The secretary never speaks and only appears on stage for two lines which the Father speaks into an imaginary telephone. 'Then cable Southampton' and 'Sixty thousand tons. Sixty.' Quite apart from the wastefulness of working as an amateur playwright and making up stories which will not get across to the audience, this way of working is likely to produce layers of unnecessary Zolaesque detail in the performance, which not only get in the way of the essentials but lead to a performance in a style alien to that of the play. It is far from being a naturalistic play. The action is meant to take place inside the hero's mind. The 'office' is a platform; the 'home' has no furniture. People sit on ledges and crevices. To a real toad in an imaginary garden, a map of a real garden is no help in making the best use of the space.

Of course an actor cannot start work on a part, any more than a director can start work on a play, by aiming straight at a style. You have to achieve a reality before you can abstract from it. But you can visualize a complete person without being completely informed about him. Just as an unrealistic portrait can tell you far more about its subject than a photograph, the actor needs to deal in broad strokes, not fiddling details, and if a characterization is to be successful, there will be the same selection in thinking about the character's background as actually in presenting him on the stage.[1]

It may well be helpful for the actor to think about things that cannot themselves be conveyed to the audience. Barry Dennen, whose characterization of the Master of Ceremonies in *Cabaret* made a very vivid impact, told an interviewer[2] that he had thought about the room the character lives in. 'I just know there's a ring of pomade round the sink. And I know what he smells like – a sick, sweet

[1] When Helen Hayes was playing Laurence Housman's Queen Victoria, one of her most famous characterizations, on Broadway, she did not read any of the biographies of the Queen, preferring to base her interpretation entirely on Housman's script. She did travel to London, though, to look at the Queen's old dresses in the Victoria and Albert Museum.

[2] Christine Sparks, *What's On in London*, July 12th, 1968.

smell, like cheap perfume.' The performance itself is anything but realistic. It draws, as no performance in a musical ever had before, on Schoenberg's technique of *Sprechstimme*. Halfway between speaking and singing, the voice slides sharply up and down the musical scale, lingering diabolically in a taunting falsetto. The make-up is grotesque with a clown-white base, twisted crimson mouth and thick false eyelashes. The character's main function is choric: he links the scenes and numbers together and in doing so epitomizes the sick spirit of Berlin night life in the manic Thirties. But Barry Dennen is brilliant in his combination of a generalized cruelty and corruption with an amused detachment, which allows him both to remain an individual and to show his attitude to the type. It is a highly unnaturalistic performance which digests a lot of realistic detail. And if this seems paradoxical, it is only because our normal theatrical practice is more naturalistic than we usually admit.

But the further the cracks spread in the Ibsen mould of playwriting, the sooner the tide is likely to turn decisively against naturalism in acting. In a Pinter play, there are very few clues indeed about the characters' off-stage biographies. The characters live in a continuous present tense and when they talk about their past, they are just as likely to be lying as telling the truth. As Pinter said himself in a programme note he wrote for the Royal Court Theatre,

> A character on the stage who can present no convincing argument or information as to his past experience, his present behaviour or his aspirations, nor give a comprehensive analysis of his motives is as legitimate and as worthy of attention as one who, alarmingly, can do all these things. The more acute the experience the less articulate its expression.

But how does this affect the actor? Can he know how a character dresses, walks, talks, listens and holds himself or balances a tea-cup without knowing something about his background?

It is surprising how little biographical information the actor needs. The ring of pomade round the sink is much more important than how much he is paying for the room or how long he has been living in it. It is possible for an actor to have quite an adequate working knowledge of the character's present attitudes, habits and relationships without postulating or knowing very much about their history. And, providing that the actor does not approach the part in a spirit of resentment at not being provided with more background information by Pinter, it is a revelation that so many questions can safely be left unanswered without sacrificing any definition in the character's onstage existence.

Pinter's *The Collection* is a play which never solves the mystery it is based on. James believes that his wife, Stella, has slept with a dress-designer called Bill when they were both staying at a hotel in Leeds. Bill, who lives with another man, Harry, amuses himself by encouraging James's suspicions and we hear several contradictory stories about what happened in Leeds – from Bill and from James, who tells Bill that Stella has told him about it, but we never find out whether she was telling him the truth, whether he is telling Bill the truth about what she said or whether Bill is telling the truth. But, surprisingly, the action succeeds in showing that what 'really' happened in Leeds hardly matters at all. What matters is the insecurities that the characters have about themselves and about each other. Harry does not trust Bill, James does not trust Stella and neither Bill nor Stella are finding fulfilment with their partners. Without going into the background of these relationships, Pinter illuminates them brilliantly in the present tense by setting all four characters' insecurities jangling.

For the actors, the problems that the regiment of unanswered questions presents are obvious, but Kenneth Haigh, who played James, has described (during a public discussion at the Royal Court Theatre) how he found everything he needed in the rhythm of the writing:

Harold's text was a puzzle to me until I began to see it in terms of the way he had written it, and this meant – oh boring things really to people listening to me saying this – but detailed night-long analysis of the lines, of their structure, of the relation of one sound against another, and the punctuation. All this unlocked for me the way in which Harold's mind had seen the character and eventually – I don't think actually I've seen it fully today, I'd love to do it again – I began to catch the savour of a particular world in which that particular man lived, and nobody else – I saw afterwards – could have seen the man in that way and – how can I put it – although I had an experience to bring such a situation – the nightmare in which those people lived, so charming to one another – it was only by losing some of my sovereignty and going to the fountain of the writer that I really got the last key in.[1]

This excitement at a loss of sovereignty is a far cry from Stanislavski's super-objective and from Vakhtangov's stress on wishing 'by order', but it is not at all far from Meyerhold. He worked under Stanislavski as an actor and, in his opinion, if the productions succeeded at all in capturing the authentic Chekhovian moods, it was because of the actors' response to the rhythm.

Whenever I call to mind this active participation of the actors of the Art Theatre in the creation of the characters and moods of *The Seagull*, I begin to understand how my firm faith in the actor as the main factor of the stage was born in me. Neither the *mise-en-scènes*, nor the crickets, nor the sound of horses' hoofs on the bridge, were instrumental in creating the *mood*; what did create it was the marvellous musical ear of the performers who caught the rhythm of Chekhov's poetry and who knew how to envelop their creations in a veil woven out of moonbeams.[2]

[1] Reported in *Encore*, No. 63.
[2] Quoted by Professor S. D. Balukhaty in his introduction to *The Seagull Produced by Stanislavski*. Dobson, 1952.

It is also quite close in spirit to the main message in Richard Boleslavski's book *The First Six Lessons in Acting*. They are very good lessons indeed but the unfortunate pupil does not get her fourth lesson (on character) until she has been a professional actress for several years. After watching her rehearse Ophelia and observing that she is playing it too much as herself, Boleslavski advises her to remember the period. She must play the girl as a courtier's daughter, curl her palm longwise to make it narrower. She must study period postures in picture galleries and watch the nuns in chapel on their Easter night procession. After doing some work along these lines, she will incorporate all sorts of elements into her performance which are representative of the social and historical type that Ophelia belongs to.

But when she starts trying to characterize Ophelia's way of thinking, Boleslavski advises her not to.

> Shakespeare did all the thinking for her. It is his mind at work which you should characterize ... If you were playing Juliet, you would only tie yourself in knots by trying to characterize the mind of a fourteen-year-old girl who is capable of saying
>
> > My bounty is as boundless as the sea,
> > My love as deep; the more I give to thee,
> > The more I have, for both are infinite.
>
> It is a question of rhythm. What the actress has to do is get the flow of words right.

Thanks mainly to Brecht – and to Joan Littlewood and Kenneth Tynan who, in their different ways, prepared the ground for his influence to infiltrate into England – our Shakespearian acting has passed a watershed in its development, and there are occasional productions by Peter Brook (*Marat-Sade* and *Oedipus*) which give us glimpses of what acting in the future could be like. But watching pre-war films, like Anthony Asquith's *Pygmalion* (1938), it is horribly striking how, outside Shakespeare and the classics, English acting style has hardly changed at all in thirty years when everything else has changed enormously. Interpretative arts are always slower to develop than creative arts but Boulez's Debussy seems much further removed from Ernest Ansermet's Debussy than Rex Harrison's Higgins from Leslie Howard's. The style in which the majority of West End comedies are played still seems to be inspired by Noel Coward and, judging from films, the farce technique of Brian Rix's company seems, in every way, more old-fashioned than that of the pre-war farceurs. By and large, we still have not caught up with Gordon Craig, who said that an actor cannot be satisfied with registering things like a camera. Peter Brook raised this question in that same discussion at the Royal Court in 1963: if Craig could simplify a forest scenically down to a single stick, does this not have some bearing on the art of acting? Why should the actor have to touch in every line and wrinkle of old age, every quaver in the voice and every joggle in the movement? Is it not possible to get the physical side down to a simple sketch, so that he can put more emphasis on something else which is part of the same reality?

How can the camera be replaced by the X-ray? Discussing his experience of understudying Olivier in *Coriolanus* at Stratford-on-Avon, Albert Finney said

> What one did learn from that is how a great actor can take the kind of peaks and the valleys of a performance, the ups and downs of a character as written and push them even further apart. He makes the climaxes higher, and he makes the depths of it lower, than you feel is possible in the text.[1]

There are ups and downs in every scene, every sequence but what is the best way of finding the rhythm of the relationship between them?

Like Strindberg's script, Sir Laurence Olivier's superb

[1] In an interview on B.B.C. Television.

performance in *The Dance of Death* gave us hardly any biographical knowledge of the character and there is no reason to think Olivier had invented any, even for himself. What matters is not how much he pays his servant but how he treats her on stage, and it was largely through his reactions to other people that he brought the Captain so compellingly to life, without elbowing us into wondering what had happened in the man's past to make him like this. It is obvious that in the deterioration of his relationship with Alice, his wife, he has both damaged her and been damaged by her, but we do not think about the past. We concentrate on husband and wife as they are now. They only exist in the present tense.

From the beginning of the play, Olivier showed the Captain oscillating between wary strategic hesitations in answering his wife's questions and violent bursts of loud brisk energy. Through his timing, he differentiated between the controlled shouts, done for effect – the parade ground manner adapted to the marital battlefield – and the moments of apoplectic vehemence. The unevenness of the pressure behind the storms also conveyed the impression that he was trying to go on believing in himself and not always succeeding. There was a beautifully timed piece of self-control when he cut quickly from a bellow to a table-talk question: 'Have you ever been in Copenhagen?' and another when he thundered at Kurt 'DON'T YOU . . .' and changed his tone in mid-sentence to go on casually 'think life's a queer thing?'

He pushed the ups and the downs of the part impressively far apart, showing clear and violent contrasts between his abjectness when defeated and his triumph when he won a round against the others, between the rallies of energy, the moments when tiredness showed through his determination to mask it and the moments when he gave in to it. He was very good in his mixture of phoney back-slapping friendliness and genuine excitement when Kurt arrived and in his air of offended innocence – like a television wrestler told off for fouling – when

Alice offered Kurt a drink. (He had been drinking himself without offering.) At the beginning, the rhythm of his drinking had helped him to register his indifference to Alice's familiar line of talk. Then it gave him momentum for the gruff jokes about their quarrels and his ever so slightly drunk imitation of her playing the piano, speaking out what he thought she was thinking about him. The effects of the drinking were there in the background of his attempts at cheerfulness and hearty familiarity with Kurt and then it had its effects in slowing his rhythm down. It became more of an effort to understand what Kurt was saying. But at the same time as blurring his reactions, it enabled him to sharpen the distinction between the different layers of his performance and to show his attitude to the act he was putting on. He grimaced to himself when Kurt was not looking, like a self-conscious actor coming out of character. But the performance was securely lodged inside the performance. Then his head nodded as he dozed off into unconsciousness at the onset of the first attack.

Each attack was quite different. In the first, he fell prostrate on the couch. The second started with a giddy fall behind the desk at the end of the dance he did to the Boyars' March. He got up defiantly but his determination crumbled into fears. 'It's coming back.' He showed a compelling mixture of pathos and proud irony – 'Pray forgive me for not being well' – both then and later, self-righteously, on an entrance. 'Forgive me if I sit down. I'm . . . a little tired.'

The third attack was in the chair and he got frightened when he saw the old woman outside with her washing, thinking she was Death. He lay down almost aggressively with his boots on – 'A soldier must always be prepared' – as if Death were an enemy to be fought. But he revived fully for a belligerent scene of threatening to bring another woman into the house. After this, he smashed up the room.

He led into it very slowly. Pensively he lit candles and

calmly put Alice's laurel wreaths on the floor and her photograph in the middle of them, but suddenly and alarmingly he smashed them by jumping on them. There was a row of photographs on the piano and he kissed one of them before sweeping them all to the ground and pounding on the piano. He gave himself time to aim before shooting at Alice's picture. He took a drink, spat it out, methodically emptied his cigars and cigarettes into the waste-paper basket and only began to get out of control as he threw bottles at the window. He was muttering as he threw away the love letters from the desk drawer and he started weeping, suffering silently at the desk. His aggressiveness was not just outward. When he struck the desk it was because it was the only way of giving release to the tension that had built up inside and this made the gesture mean more than much more violent external actions might have meant. He walked quite slowly to the window and tore the curtain open on one side. He went out on to the balcony laughing hysterically and he came back nursing a cat, to cross the stage with a choked sob and go up the stairs. We heard a groan and the sequence ended with an off-stage door-slam.

Certainly, like Weigel's performance in *Mother Courage*, Olivier tells us a huge amount about the human being that he is playing, but much of it is generalized. Both performances show us things that are peculiar to this private individual – things about the sensation of being alive and the fear of age and aloneness, pangs of jealousy, spasms of rage. Both performances make the characters extremely vivid but the impact does not depend in the least on individualizing by drawing an outline around a collection of characteristics. There is more stress on the inconsistency of the actions and reactions than on their consistency – this is partly how both characters are defined – and while both performances are astonishingly rich in realistic detail, it is not the sort of detail that could have been accumulated by asking questions like 'What is it in this person's personality structure or past experience that makes him (or her) different from everyone else?' Part of the reason both performances are so moving is that we can all see ourselves in them.

///

7 · COUNTERPOINT AND TIMING

According to Coquelin, the actor must avoid reproducing character traits which are purely individual.

> The actor must take care not to adopt the characteristics of some special miser whom he may know but whom the public does not know, but instead he should give, as Harpagon, the concentrated essence of all misers, which his audience would recognize instantly.[1]

This approach would be quite unacceptable today. A character would be dismissed as a type or caricature if the actor concentrated entirely on his dominant trait like this. Lee Strasberg tells the story of how Stanislavski had to push the actor Leonidev away from playing just miserliness.

> So Stanislavski said, 'Don't worry about playing a miser. Try playing the man as if he really wanted to do everything possible for everybody. When a man comes into your place and you have to say, I'll give you something, try to look around and find what you could give him. Really try to find something to give him, but discover that actually you can't find anything that's good enough . . . . . ., so that you end up by not giving him anything.' Thus, Leonidev got away from obvious miserliness. There was something that made him miserly, but at the same time,

[1] *Actors on Acting*, Cole and Chinoy.

if someone accused him of being a miser, he would say, 'What do you mean? You're crazy,' and he would be perfectly justified in his own thinking in combating the idea.[1]

It is important to remember, though, that Stanislavski intended this as a corrective of what Leonidev was doing. It would be easy for an actor to go too far in the direction of playing the character from his own point of view and lose the playwright's critical perspective on him, as with the murderers in *Richard III*, where the actors need to show us both the corruption of a society in which men could make a living by hiring themselves out as killers and the casualness of the professionals who take killing very much as a matter of course.

Of contemporary directors, Peter Brook has been the one to force actors and audiences to abandon their old, entrenched moral position in relation to Shakespeare's best known characters. Under his direction, Alec Clunes played Claudius in *Hamlet* (1955) with a sympathy which has influenced many subsequent Claudiuses and in Brook's *Lear*, the King's petulance and the rowdyism of his knights went some way towards justifying Goneril's and Regan's initial reactions, while Kent and Gloucester were submitted to a similar moral revaluation, showing up in a far less favourable light than usual.

The principle of looking for the opposite element is a sound one. Both in large leading parts and small supporting parts, there will always be a trait or traits that seem to be dominant. Coquelin's Molièresque approach may have been right for an audience that took pleasure in categorizing vices and virtues and tying labels to the packages of human behaviour that were presented to it on the stage, but today we want to get as far away as possible from 'types'. Our diet is richer and our palates are more jaded. Seeing a play is no longer a special social event. We can see two in an evening by

[1] *Strasberg at the Actors' Studio*, ed. Robert H. Hethmon. Cape.

turning a knob. And if the playwright produces a type, as he often does, it is up to the actor to dig out the opposite elements. We have had so many typical secretaries, typical shop-girls, typical landladies offered to us on stage, in films and television, that it makes us very much less willing to believe there is any such thing as a typical secretary, a typical shop-girl or a typical landlady. So we get very bored with actresses who fail to find traits to carry the character at least a few yards away from the hypothetical norm, however small the part is.

The worse a play is, the more the director and actors have to do the playwright's job for him. In Claudius, Goneril and Gloucester, Shakespeare wrote in the counterpoint and it is up to the conductors and the individual performers to reinterpret it, deciding how hard to strike each note. In inferior plays the notes are not there in the script and the actor has to write them in.

It is striking how many of the individual moments in acting performances that leave a mark on the memory do so because of the way they either strike discords or modulate sharply between two notes which could have caused a discord if touched together. If the essence of drama is conflict, the conflict can sometimes be meaningfully expressed in a single moment in which the protagonist holds on to both halves of an opposition. No one who saw the Kozintsev film of *Hamlet* will forget the play scene in which the King, showing the strain but remembering where he is, starts clapping before he breaks down and calls for lights. And in Frank Dunlop's production of the Brecht version of Marlowe's *Edward II* at the National Theatre, the murder was far more terrifying because the murderer, Lightborn (Graham Crowden) was so tender and reassuring. After the coldness of Mortimer's behaviour, the warmth of Lightborn was almost enough to make us forget his reason for coming to the prison. The businesslike way he donned his apron and asked the gaoler for what he needed – a table and a feather bed – were dramatically at odds with the sympathetic tone he adopted with the King (John Stride) and with the undisguised homosexual pleasure at physical contact with him. He offered him peace, rest, a bed and Edward leaned back wearily, gratefully against him, lulled. His hands went under the King's arms supporting him from behind and caressing his chest. After helping him gently on to the bed, he placed the table upside down on top of him, leaped up on it and danced about fiercely, crushing the hard board into Edward's ribs. But even now in the dancing movement there was something that contradicted the idea of killing, rather in the way that two antitheses were 'yoked by violence together' in Metaphysical poetry.

Weak kings have been recurrent figures in drama because of the contrast that they embody – a contrast Michael Chekhov seems to have captured well when he played Strindberg's Eric XIV at the First Studio of the Moscow Art Theatre. Here is Robert Lewis's description of one moment from the performance which Chekhov repeated long afterwards in a lecture to demonstrate a 'psychological gesture'. It was a moment when the King had to give an order.

> And when he gave the order with his hand, his wrist then went limp in a very weak, effeminate way, and he became a little frightened at the sound of his own voice. So the combination of this King's wish to give an order and manifest his kingliness, and the limp wrist and the fright at the sound of his own voice, created a marvellous image of the weak king.[1]

It is not often possible to contain the valley and the peak in a single gesture like this, but we ought to be more aware than we are of the way stage business can work as counterpoint. The fact that the actor is *doing* something, besides talking and listening, divides his attention, and instead of

[1] Robert Lewis in an interview in the *Tulane Drama Review*, Vol. 9, No. 2.

weakening his concentration, the simultaneous pull in two directions strengthens it. The fact of having something to do is also helpful not just in providing an alternative to sitting or standing around but in providing an extra language of expression. You can convey a mood by the way you slam a suitcase shut or show your reaction to someone else by the way you turn your head and straighten your back as you break off from your packing. The actor is always in a position of advantage when there are two possible objects for his attention and energy: the way he divides them between the two then becomes meaningful.

To take a very simple example, there is a scene towards the end of the musical *Fiddler on the Roof* when the Jews are all being driven out of the town by a pogrom and Tevye, the milkman-hero, who has packed all his possessions together ready to leave, is strapping up a basket. One of his daughters who has married a Gentile, comes to say goodbye and to ask his forgiveness. She stands upstage of him; he is bending down over the basket and apparently gives his whole attention to the business of fastening it in order to keep his face averted from her as she moves around him trying to make him look at her. The movements of his hands vary, now brisk, now fumbling, now savage, so that without saying a word and without even looking up, he can express his mixed feelings towards the daughter he loved who has now married one of the enemy. It is a very good piece of business and when Alfie Bass took over the part he played it in almost exactly the same way as Topol had.

Sometimes the dramatist writes in business which suggests a play of opposites. In *Three Sisters*, the scent that Soliony keeps rubbing into his hands makes us aware that they are sweaty and smelly. Lady Macbeth's business of wringing her hands as if washing them makes her mental image of the blood on them real for us. Hedda Gabler's business with the pistols plants an important question mark about where, for her, the borderline between game and reality is situated, and in Strindberg's *The Father* the business of getting the Captain into his straitjacket is made emotionally far more complex by the fact that it is his old nurse who lulls him into submission. The safe games of the nursery are recalled in an ugly, contrasting context.

More often, though, it is left to the director and the actor to invent what business is needed. In Peter Brook's production of the *Marat-Sade* there was a brilliantly effective scene where Charlotte Corday (Glenda Jackson) used her hair to whip the Marquis de Sade. This was Glenda Jackson's idea; Peter Brook filled it out and integrated it into the production by getting the surrounding crowd of lunatics to make whistling sounds like a whip slicing through the air and groans as the 'whip' hit de Sade. Again the theatrical effectiveness depended on an almost Metaphysical coupling of opposites thoroughly appropriate to de Sade, tenderness and cruelty, intimacy and aggression, pleasure and pain.

If proof were needed of the importance of business in the theatre, it would be provided by the productions that try to do without it. William Gaskill's *Macbeth* at the Royal Court in November 1966 is a case in point. Inspired, perhaps, by the Beckett of *Happy Days* it had brilliant light pouring unremittingly down on a square bare sandbox of a set (Banquo got a laugh in the line 'There's husbandry in heaven. Their candles are all out!'). Forced down to the fore of the Royal Court's small stage and stranded there without any help from props, furniture, atmosphere or interaction with the rest of the cast, all the protagonists could do was speak their lines rather like audition pieces. There was some good speaking, but very little acting, even from Sir Alec Guinness.

One reason an actor needs business is that timing is one of his main weapons and he is too restricted in the use of it if he has nothing to time except his lines. Another advantage of expressing feelings through business, as Tevye does in strapping up the basket, is that variations in the rhythm of the action look involuntary. When an actor is dividing himself between what he is saying (or hearing) and what he is doing, it is not difficult to control the shifts of energy and attention between one and the other in a way that seems uncontrolled. And the more that acting seems to consist in reacting, the more spontaneous it will look.

Everything depends on the timing but the word timing (like so many of our key words) is misleading because it suggests a deliberate gauging of split seconds. In fact, although the actor is partly conscious of the rhythm that he is letting his actions respond to, he could not achieve the same results by calculation. In *On Actors and the Art of Acting* G. H. Lewes tells a story about a girl Voltaire was coaching. She gesticulated so much and so uncontrollably that he had to resort to making her recite with her hands tied to her side. She started off quietly, but soon, carried away, she flung out her arms forcibly enough to snap the threads. Aghast, she apologized. But Voltaire was delighted with her. The irrepressible gesture had been a good one, as irrepressible gestures usually are. If Voltaire had told her in advance to do the gesture two beats ahead of a particular phrase, he would have ruined both the gesture and the phrase.

Every pause has its ideal length – even though the ideal length would vary slightly from performance to performance – and you are mistiming if you depart from it by so much as a split second. This is not to say that it is always right to come in with your line or reaction on the crest of the pause – the moment at which it is most natural. Sometimes a comic effect depends upon speeding up the natural reaction, sometimes on retarding it. Often, the meaning of a line varies according to whether an actor speaks it on the crest of the pause, or before, or after, or how much before or after. When Hamlet, at the end of the nunnery speech, suddenly asks Ophelia 'Where's your father?' and she, knowing that he is eavesdropping on them, replies 'At home, my lord', she tells us how easy or difficult it is for her to tell a direct lie by the speed with which she picks up her cue.

Sometimes, particularly in comedy, a deflationary line needs to be pricked into the pause right on its crest. There was an example of this in David Storey's play *The Restoration of Arnold Middleton* when Arnie was standing on his head to show off in front of a visitor and after ignoring him for a time, Joan, his wife looked at him directly, paused, and offered him a cup of tea.

In the film *Accident* when Stephen (Dirk Bogarde) and Anna (Jacqueline Sassard) go out for a walk in the country, there is a silence when his hand is resting a few inches away from hers on the top of the gate. We know that it must be decided now whether the mutual attraction between them is going to grow into anything positive. She has avoided the others to come out with him and if he fails to take his chance now, he probably never will. It would be very easy to move his hand a couple of inches to touch hers. He doesn't. How long the pause lasts before the line 'Shall we go back now?' is crucial to our assessment of his assessment of the chance he's throwing up.

There is no saying what the right length is for any of these three crucial pauses, except in relation to the performance.

The rhythm of a performance is something you will be able to find from the words – if the script is good enough – but once you have found it, it is the same rhythm that conditions your movements, your pauses, the way you listen and the way you react, or fail to react. It is like a pulse in the bloodstream of the part. It is this that gives you the feeling that the character is using you and that you cannot go wrong.

Not that the part itself can absolutely determine the rhythm, which is affected by a whole nexus of relationships – between the part, the actor's personality, the other parts, the other personalities, the set, the production style and so on. Dame Edith Evans and Lila Kedrova have both given excellent performances as Madam Ranevsky in *The Cherry Orchard* but the two characterizations were totally different, especially in rhythm. Dame Edith adapted her majestic rubato to produce a fairly composed surface, cratered with wounds, and she flooded it with warmth at unexpected moments when the feeling welled up from underneath. Lila Kedrova's rhythm was much less dignified. Her highly charged ebullient personality conveyed the feeling that, like certain liquids, she had a fairly low boiling point. Enthusing over her performance critics made a lot of the argument that a Slav has an innate advantage over an English actress in playing a Russian part. But Dame Edith made a far better Madam Ranevsky than Tarassova, who played it when the Moscow Art Theatre came to Sadler's Wells.

Laughter came easily to Kedrova in sudden shrieks and tinkles and she seemed delighted by so many things that happened around her, just as her pretty, ravaged face gave every sign of having enjoyed the experiences that ravaged it. She was irresistibly charming when she was pleading, but she did not hide the self-pity behind the mixture of fear and anger and pressured defiance when Madam Ranevsky declared her love for the man in Paris. Like Dame Edith's, her personality is rich enough to afford its openness to the play of impulse – at the end, for instance, when she could not bear to leave the house and insisted on staying inside it just one minute longer.

Kedrova was positively frisky when Lopahin, after her appeal to him, consented to marry Varya and because her basic rhythm was so animated, she was particularly effective in her moments of stillness. Failing to respond to a stimulus can be just as positively meaningful as responding to it and she did this, very tellingly, twice. The first time was in Act One when Trofimov came in, all keyed up for the meeting, and confronted with his excitement, she did not react at all. She knew that she knew him and she stood like an animal trapped in a beam of light, frightened, on guard. Then at the first mention of Grisha, her dead son, she gave a big sob as she identified Trofimov as his ex-tutor and half stumbling, half running, she threw herself into his arms. The second time was when Lopahin was describing the auction of the cherry orchard. The neighbours crowded round him avidly, listening too hard, reacting too much, too sycophantically. With her back half turned away, she reacted by not reacting at all. It was a moment not unlike Weigel's inhibition of emotion when she had to identify the body of Mother Courage's second son.

Obviously, neither actress would have timed these non-reactions mechanically but the technique is a serious counterpart to the traditional comic device of the delayed reaction. Laurel and Hardy often used it. A character hits another hard over the head and instead of falling he goes on talking as if nothing has happened. A few moments later he falls. The well known 'double take' is similar. The actor reacts to a line without having taken in its full meaning. He turns away, takes it in and turns back with a different reaction.

Actors can learn a lot from watching comedians. Paul Scofield's performance in *Staircase* must have owed a good deal to Frankie Howerd. Brecht, who greatly admired Chaplin, wrote a scene into *Arturo Ui* which derives directly from *The Great Dictator*, and Ekkehard Schall incorporated some adroitly Chaplinesque clowning into his performance in the main part. Olivier says that he watches all his colleagues for different qualities and imitates them unashamedly. The comedian he borrowed from most was Sid Field and the actor he used to watch for timing was Rex Harrison.

Olivier's performance in *The Dance of Death* was a model of good timing and it is worth going back to the scene in which he smashes up the room because it offers a comparison with an almost identical scene in John Mortimer's play *The Judge*. Returning to the town where he lived as a young man, the Judge finds that the woman he loved still lives there. Failing to get any emotional change out of her, he smashes up her living-room. Like Strindberg's Captain, he has been drinking heavily but there was an enormous difference between Patrick Wymark's hysteria as the Judge and Olivier's as

the Captain. Patrick Wymark gave an energetic performance, building up great momentum and then taking everything
into his stride, like a demolition worker gone berserk. Olivier
also put a lot of energy into what he did, but he did not let it
come out in an even flow and he always kept something in
reserve. He was under great tension but never let the character get too far out of control to think between each action and
move forward to the next on the crest of the pause. Each
action in the room smashing episode stood out individually
because he gave it time to grow out of the previous one and
the whole sequence grew out of everything that had gone
before it.

It was a matter mainly of timing. Wymark forgot the
reculer pour mieux sauter. Olivier remembered it and balanced
the violence by finding points of softness all through the scene
(like kissing Alice's photograph and reacting to the love letters). This helped him to show that the violence was directed
partly against himself. Altogether, he brought off the very
difficult feat of making the Captain sufficiently out of control
to break up the room and sufficiently under control to take
time over doing so. Both Wymark's character and his actual
handling of himself in the part were far closer to being out of
control and the scene showed how meaningless violent action
can be without good timing. There needs to be either counterpoint inside the flow of actions or contrast with something
outside.

8 · WASTE OF ACTORS

Writing about problems of technique in acting, I inevitably
find myself writing chiefly about actors for whom technique

is no longer a problem. But the vast majority of actors in England do not play one challenging lead after another, and technique, unfortunately, is something which shrinks unless it is constantly stretched.

Like any other artist, an actor can always do more than he thinks he can and he is only working at his best when he is taxing his resources, exploring, digging deeper, discovering new areas. The talented beginner who does well at a good drama school finishes his training with something of a technique but unless he is lucky in the jobs he gets, it immediately starts to deteriorate. It is not a knack you can never lose, like riding a bicycle. There are parts which stretch an actor by taking him through a wide variety of emotional states and making him react to a wide variety of situations. And there are parts which stretch him because he would have thought them outside his range if the directors were not there to egg him on. Nothing is so bad for the actor as specializing in one kind of part, and, unfortunately, the larger an industry, the greater the pressure towards specialization. The English film and television industries are both large and both crowded with producers, directors and casting directors who are too unimaginative or too insecure in their positions to take any risks. They play safe by using actors in the same kind of parts they have used them in before or seen them in before.

The result is that for most of their working lives, most of our actors have to choose between being steadily underpaid in provincial repertory to play parts which are on the verge of being outside their range or being unsteadily overpaid in films and television to play parts which are all too safely within their range. In theory they can divide themselves between the two kinds of job but in practice, wives, flats, agents, habit, unpaid bills and a Micawberish optimism about the break around the corner keep most of them in London most of the time, working only occasionally in the theatre and living alternately off television and the dole. Singers can practise, dancers can do classes and, in New York, actors can do classes but for the victim of type-casting in London, there is no way of keeping in training.

It is not even as though playing a small part in a small play on the small screen gave the actor a chance of 'playing himself'. In *Building a Character* Stanislavski distinguishes between two types of cliché in acting. There are actors 'who hold the public through their original ways, their finely wrought special variety of acting clichés' and there are actors who borrow clichés from other actors instead of working out their own. Television is rich in both kinds of cliché but it is the first kind which is the major pitfall for the talented beginner. Working in an atmosphere of pressure and insecurity and knowing he got the part because of his performance in another play, the temptation to repeat at least something of that performance is highly insidious. If it was one that depended on particular physical features, personality traits or mannerisms, he starts to rely on them. If he used tricks, he starts to repeat them. Soon he is imitating himself. The inventiveness he started with begins to dry up. He is being paid to repeat himself, not to explore himself. Eventually he stops being an artist and becomes a businessman trading in his appearance and mannerisms. (It would be interesting to know when the phrase 'Are you in the business?' started to be used between actors.)

Not that the small-part actor in the Royal Shakespeare Company or the National Theatre is necessarily all that much better off. The best documentation on this under-ventilated subject was provided by the magazine *Encore* when it published *Diary of a Small-part Actor* by Michael Murray.

Actors who succeed in a small part are: (1) those who know the *exact* value of what they're doing and do it, neither more nor less, and who don't overvalue themselves in a small part; (2) those who don't seem to care and are therefore relaxed, suggesting a real person on the stage and not a cardboard copy of a person; (3) those who come on the stage looking as though they've *come* from somewhere and go off as if they're *going* somewhere. One must also know how to 'paint' a scene like an artist, know what stroke to make and how to make it boldly. Trouble is there never seems enough time in a production to work this out in detail.

Michael Murray's main complaint is that most of the time it is impossible to relax or concentrate on the part in the hurly-burly of competing with other small-part actors to get noticed by the director.

Make yourself obvious and he'll choose you for some bit of business. Try to be first on and last off and they'll notice you. Push and shove. Shout louder than anyone else etc.

The diary also describes how he nearly came to blows with another actor because both were using the same tricks to make the most out of their first entrances.

I try to keep the audience's attention by resorting to 'follow-through' stuff (attaching gesture to beginning and end of speeches as a sort of prologue and epilogue – hand-kerchief-waving, which signals to the audience 'This is me, I am about to speak', 'That was me, I have spoken.')

This is technique misused.

Most large-cast productions waste the talents of most of the actors playing in them for most of the time. One of the reasons that Peter Brook's production of Seneca's *Oedipus* was so exciting was that it didn't. All thirty-six actors had their energy and their concentration involved for most of the time and each one of them, including Sir John Gielgud and Irene Worth, was having his technique extended by being made to do things he had never done before.

As the audience came in to find lights shining on a huge gold cube rotating in the centre of the stage, the actors had already started assembling in black rehearsal clothes as if to take part in a rite, some on stage and some in the auditorium at picked vantage points in the stalls and both circles, most of them leaning against the metal pillars, sitting or standing on the specially built wooden perches with a small spotlight on each of them. Signalled by a rap from on stage, a low humming started, coming very softly from all of them, a single note from the stage and all over the auditorium, which grew louder and grew into a harmony. But there was something unfamiliar about the quality of the hum. During the ten weeks of rehearsals, for three of which they had worked without scripts, Peter Brook had played records of Tibetan monks resonating and done exercises with the actors to get them to resonate, as singers can, from the chest.

Then the beating began, the on-stage actors beating with their hands on their gold-clad wooden boxes, the others beating against their pillars, while the light on the slowly turning gold cube grew in intensity, making it throw painful searchlight beams into the faces of the audience. As the patting hands reached a crescendo, the three leading actors made their entrance and took up positions facing away from the audience towards the gold cube.

'Sh-sh-sh.' The sound started off all over the theatre, gradually growing into the word 'Show'. 'Show us a simple riddle' one voice said clearly, and immediately other voices took it up, breaking it up, repeating fragments and then going on into the first chorus. 'Huh!' The sound comes and comes repeatedly from Philip Locke, one of the chorus leaders, as he slices the air with a vicious knifelike downward movement of his flat hand, and this is used as punctuation as a single voice describes how the plague is hitting Thebes. Oedipus's first speech is transposed from much farther on in Seneca's script and it capsules the whole story so that, in this production, he is not ignorant of what is going to happen to him. At the end of the first section of his speech, we get the 'Huh' all through his lines, producing a pressure behind his rhythm and suggesting the involvement of the citizens in the fate of their King. Gielgud afterwards said on television that it was like being supported as a solo voice is by the chorus in an oratorio.

After listening in silence to the first part of his speech to the gods, they come in with a heavy, loud, rhythmic, deep breathing which is used again as backing to part of Jocasta's first speech. The next chorus is split up between single voices, some on stage, some in the auditorium, which has the effect of making the things which are only being narrated – not even enacted – seem to be happening all round us. A loud sound, half way between a swallow and a groan, punctuates the lamentations. Then 'Tckkk', dry clicking sounds start as concerted punctuation for individual speaking voices.

A hollow rhythmic group laugh comes after each line denying the gods. There are some sung notes here, and some sounds like the sounds Noh actors make. Some of the on-stage actors go into poses: one man stands like a spent swimmer. The chorus now start breaking up their lines more than ever, repeating phrases and overlapping with each other. Which words you hear most clearly depend on where you are sitting in the auditorium but behind the blur of sound, the sense is clear.

'I didn't know what terror was, I feel it now as I speak.' Creon (Colin Blakely) makes this a perfectly flat statement but the general atmosphere of terror has been so well substantiated that there is no need for him to emote. But when he quotes what the oracle said at the shrine, he uses a high pitched monotone, speaking against a background of humming.

As the blind Tiresias (Frank Wylie) makes his entrance, we hear 'Ksssh' and 'Pssst' noises, and a sound like a whip whistling through the air as he speaks. It continues as he interrogates his daughter Manto (Louise Purnell). Their faces are expressionless, solemn. Her delivery is flat, with the alarm held in behind it. When he acts out the embarrassment of the gods, who themselves cannot speak out, the chorus produces a stylized equivalent of the helpless sounds a dumb man makes. The noises grow louder, faster, a groaning grunting humming which takes on a rapid sexy rhythm mounting to a climax of excitement.

On the cue 'Let the men sing' we get the chorus speaking in unison for the first time. One of the group conducts with his arm and an urgent rhythm is produced by stamping, tapping, shrieking and inarticulate sounds. Jocasta comes to the fore again on the line 'the Queen and her womb'. With Oedipus cowering almost in a foetal position, Irene Worth thuds across the whole width of the stage in a strange, straddling gait, legs stiffly spread, knees bent but rigid, her hands on them, doing a half-turn with each awkward stride. Inside the open gold cube, Creon crawls round on his belly, thumping the floor like an angry baby and shouting like an imperious man.

The colloquy between Oedipus and Jocasta is spoken with them both lying flat on separate sloping sides of the opened box, suggesting a sleepless night and a shared waking nightmare. When one of the chorus describes the voyage we get sounds from the rest of them like a bosun's whistle, and, for the Icarus speech, uncanny aerial sounds, evocative of the vastness of empty space.

Ronald Pickup plays the messenger who describes how Oedipus blinds himself. He breaks the lines into short phrases, ending them all on the same note and then gradually raises the note to a higher level. The declamation is flat, but pain and bitterness tear savagely into the restrained sound, and the breaks in the flow of sound themselves become expressive. Like Weigel in 1929 when she had to announce Jocasta's death, he makes the bare facts of what has happened more moving than any show of emotion possibly could be. But he cannot help his hands from rising in front of his eyes when he comes to the actual blinding. And then again he is simply reporting facts, like Brecht's witness of the street accident, when he says 'Blood came spouting out over his face and head. In a moment he was drenched.' Not the least impressive thing about Ronald Pickup's performance is the hiatus with which he ends it. His exit is a carefully planned anti-climax, an eloquent silence which has the effect of a shrug. As if to say 'What can you do?'

After Tiresias has fixed the black eye-patches which denote blindness on Oedipus's face, Gielgud holds his head stiffly, as if he is now estranged from it and moves pathetically, tentatively. He stands frozen like a tree as Jocasta moves towards the erect golden spike which has now been fixed into the floor of the open cube, representing Oedipus's sword. 'Turn your head towards me,' she entreats. 'Show me your face.' He barely moves as he tells her to go away. She goes on speaking in the same broken cadences, but the body has drained out of her voice, leaving it hoarse and hollow, and she finds the same rhythm vocally, punching out the broken cadences, that she used for her straddling swinging walk across the stage.

The actual impaling was different the second time I saw it (July 1968) from when the production opened in March. It was better in March, and simpler. She stood about a foot away from the spike but played as if it were going into her body. As in Glenda Jackson's business of using her hair as a whip, there was a strong sado-masochistic element here. The golden spike is as much a phallus as a sword and her groans as she impales herself have satisfaction in them as well as pain. It is a fierce and exciting struggle to achieve the climax of death, although in July she was elaborating too much on the deep throaty groaning gasps by introducing high pitched sounds, like grace notes, on each grating indrawn breath. She dies erect and open-mouthed.

The production ends with a modern bacchanalian revel. Led by a six-piece band playing a raucous tune, the cast – some in golden animal masks, all with golden carnival cloaks over their black clothes – dance through the auditorium and round the huge golden phallus which has replaced the spike on the stage. As they strip off their gold cloaks, the dancing gets wilder. The effect is extremely funny but you know, if you feel like laughing, that it is the release of the extraordinary tension of the last two hours.

Altogether, it is astonishing how deeply the production has drawn on the resources of the actors and it is a reminder of how much more could be achieved in the theatre if only directors would make more use of what actors can do. I am not suggesting that this production style would be appropriate to every play, but it shows how little the average director demands of the average actor – hardly enough to let him flex his technical muscles.

It would have been interesting to see how Peter Brook would have handled *The Tempest* if he had gone on to produce it after using it as a basis for exercises with a group of actors from different countries. They started working in Paris for the 1968 Théâtre des Nations and continued (after the students' rebellion) at the Round House in London. On the basis of the four performances they gave in front of an audience, it was hard to believe that Peter Brook's new approach would have allowed the balance between words and physical action to settle satisfactorily. It was good to see him exploring the no-man's land between mime and drama, and making the actors experiment to find out how much they could express through their bodies and through sounds that have nothing to do with words – humming, resonating, groaning and so on. Some of the lines were chanted, some repeated again and again ritualistically and a Japanese actor beautifully evoked the wind with a sound made in Noh drama while the others reacted to this imagined tempest with huddled body-movements and whimpering noises. But the conflict between Prospero and Caliban was shifted on to an ineptly physical level and it was absurd to make Prospero swing athletically by one arm from the top of some scaffolding during a narrative speech. It was not the dangling actor's fault that the words he shouted out were almost meaningless. The physical action prevented him from thinking.

Two of the main influences on Brook have been Antonin

Artaud and Jerzy Grotowski. Although Artaud was a poet, he was violently anti-literary and he formed and formulated his theories about theatre after watching a performance – which he completely misunderstood – by a group of Balinese dancers at the Colonial Exhibition of 1931. Actually the gestures of the dancers were signs which each had a specific meaning, even if it was only comprehensible to the Balinese, but he took them to be cosmic gestures to evoke superior powers. The performance left him wanting to uproot the theatre of words and personal relationships and to replace it with a theatre of extreme action, a theatre of myth and magic in which the spectator could be furnished

> with the truthful precipitate of dreams, in which his taste for crime, his erotic obsessions, his savagery, his chimeras, his utopian sense of life and matter, even his cannibalism pour out on a level not counterfeit and illusory, but interior.

Without wanting to suppress speech altogether, he wanted to give it a much smaller role and, at the same time, to restore its spellbinding power, which meant, in practice, recourse to a chanting designed to work almost hypnotically. But the play was to depend primarily on

> cries, groans, apparitions, surprises, theatricalities of all kinds, magic beauty of costumes taken from certain ritual models, resplendent lighting, incantational beauty of voices, the charms of harmony, rare notes of music, colours of objects, physical rhythm of movements whose crescendo and decrescendo will accord exactly with the pulsation of movements familiar to everyone, concrete appearances of new and surprising objects, masks, effigies yards high, sudden changes of light . . . [1]

Despite the revival of interest in his ideas and in his phrase

[1] Antonin Artaud, *The Theatre and Its Double*, translated by Mary Caroline Richards. Grove Press.

'The Theatre of Cruelty', the only play of Artaud's to have
been revived in London is *A Spurt of Blood* which Peter Brook
and Charles Marowitz staged in their *Theatre of Cruelty* at the
LAMDA Theatre. The minimal dialogue, the noises, the
sensationalist violence and the oversized symbols only produced the wrong sort of embarrassment in the audience and
the wrong sort of laughter.

Grotowski is a more realistic theatrical practitioner who
also wants theatre to depend less on words but he is even more
averse to spectacular effects. Believing that theatre cannot
compete with the visual refinements of cinema and television,
he is dedicated to the idea of a Poor Theatre, reduced to a
simple, uncluttered relationship between performer and spectator, without make-up, without lighting effects, without
even a stage. The actor who is primarily concerned with
applause, personal success, personal charm and salary he
compares with a courtesan. The actors in his Teatr Labora-
torium undergo a rigorous physical and vocal training but
instead of teaching them to accumulate skills, the object of
the method is to eliminate everything that encourages cliché
and prevents them from giving themselves in a spirit of love
and self-sacrifice. 'The body must be freed from all resist-
ance,' Grotowski says. 'It must virtually cease to exist.'[1] In
training, the actor must neither live his role nor detach himself from it but use it like a surgeon's scalpel to cut through
to the inside of his own personality, to expose it and sacrifice
it. (Sacrifice is a key word.)

The playwright's text is subordinate in importance to the
moment of encounter with the audience. Grotowski produced *Dr Faustus* by rearranging Marlowe's sequence of
scenes, suppressing some scenes and writing in others. The
role of Mephistopheles, who became androgynous, was divided between an actor and an actress. His production of
The Constant Prince was intended to bear the same relation to
Calderon's text as a variation does to an unoriginal theme in

[1] Jerzy Grotowski, *Towards a Poor Theatre*. Odin Teatrets Forlag.

music. His production of *Akropolis* took still greater liberties with Wyspianski's script.

Nevertheless, there is much that the English theatre could learn from Grotowski, particularly from his method of training actors. Whether or not we have too much respect for the text, we certainly have too little respect for the body, too little interest in exploring it, developing it, expressing ourselves through it. The body has means of thinking independently of the mind and this is something our theatre barely uses.

Grotowski teaches his actors not to regard the voice as something separate from the body. They learn to resonate simultaneously from the front of the head and the chest and to use the larynx, the nose, the occiput, the back of the jaws, the abdomen and even parts of the spine. This means that much more of the body is involved in the business of producing a sound and this degree of physical commitment can facilitate the process of opening out. The more naturally expressive the body is, the more natural all expression becomes, and Grotowski aims at a sincerity in performance which in our theatre is seldom achieved. Actions like killing, for instance, are staged with a theatrical flourish but he encourages his actors to draw on intimate memories – perhaps of an internal struggle over killing an animal – which may be very difficult to re-enact. The actor must neither play for himself nor for the audience. He must remain internally passive but externally active. 'His search must be directed from within himself *to* the outside but not *for* the outside. . . . The problem is always the same: stop the cheating, find the authentic impulses.'[1]

What we need to find is a new balance between speech and action, mind and body. It may be that neither Brook nor Grotowski has yet found it, but we shall need far more experiments of the kind they have been making before we can overcome our fear of the physical. And then we may find a way of using our bodies more without sacrificing the words.

[1] Jerzy Grotowski, *Towards a Poor Theatre*.

In the meanwhile, there is perhaps a cue to be taken from Ingmar Bergman's production of *Hedda Gabler* which showed, without doing any violence to the text, that there is no need to be shackled by the conventional structure of plays in the Ibsen tradition. Bergman did away with the realistic parlour set, painted all his walls a passionate red, dispensed with most of the furniture, and coloured the rest the same red, introduced an extra room into the set and kept Hedda on-stage a lot of the time she is normally off. This gives the actress a chance to show how she behaves when she is on her own – pacing silently, idly, like a caged panther, bored, eaves-dropping on the fatuous family chat going on in the parlour. The husband, Tesman, a fussy bourgeois bore, is rather like Helmer in *The Doll's House*, and the scenes without Hedda, which today normally seem far too leisurely in their exposi-tion and far too blunt in their satire, gain enormously from having Hedda's reactions to them as an obbligato accompani-ment. This is the only point of comparison with Peter Brook's *Oedipus*: both productions bring in the reactions of characters whose reactions would normally be left out of the picture.

I hesitate to make a McLuhanite point at this stage of the argument, but it is relevant that the audience's eye has been educated by the visual media to take in more information more quickly. The theatre does not have to compete with multi-screen techniques in the cinema, but most members of most audiences would feel that Ibsen's exposition of the plot in *The Doll's House* and *Hedda Gabler* is much too slow, and hundreds of other, later plays written in the same mould suffer from the same fault. The basic material of the best of these plays is still valid but naturalistic production and acting can no longer select the right points at the right speed to present to the audience in the right way. It is time for new styles and new techniques.

9 · ACTING FOR THE CAMERA

George Jean Nathan once said that an actor's performance on the screen bore the same relation to a performance on the stage that a hiccup bears to Camille's tuberculosis. We shall need to go into the relationship more fully.

Different techniques are involved in acting for the camera because the demands made on the actor are totally different. There are different stimuli, different restrictions, different areas of freedom within them. The microphone and the camera remove all problems of filling a space. You have no difficulty in making yourself heard when there is a microphone following you about on a boom, sensitive enough to pick up the smallest sound you can produce, and obviously it is an advantage that the slightest motion of a cheek muscle or a twitch at the corner of your mouth can be easily visible. (The disadvantage for the actor who is experienced in theatre work and inexperienced in films and television is that he has to inhibit instincts he has developed in the course of accustoming himself to filling large spaces.) Another advantage is that the whole audience is seeing exactly the same performance, whereas in the theatre you know you are giving something different to the stockbroker in the stalls from what you are giving to the student who is fifty yards away in the gallery, looking down on you at a steep angle.

So the cinema can use actors who lack projection. Democratically, it also blunts the impact of a powerful personality. It is meaningless to speak of one actor's having more 'presence' than another on the screen. Some will catch the eye more readily than others, simply because their appearance is more eye-catching but it is no longer up to the actor to draw the audience's attention to him. In the theatre, an actor fills only a tiny proportion of the space that is visible to the audience. Even to a man in the front stalls – unless he is using opera glasses, in which case he is approximating to the conditions of cinema – the nearest actor looks much smaller than he would in a film close-up and most of the visible space is filled by the set. In the cinema, the camera can take the audience's attention wherever the director wants it. It is not up to the actor to make sure the audience notices that he is putting the letter in his left-hand jacket pocket; if the camera is on him they cannot miss it. It is also possible, in effect, for the director to use actors as scenery. *Et Dieu Créa la Femme* was more or less an admiring travelogue about most of the areas of Brigitte Bardot's body and Truffaut has defined cinema as the art of photographing beautiful women. Even in an undisputed work of art like Eisenstein's *Ivan the Terrible* much depends on using the actor as scenery – the actual faces Eisenstein chose, the way he lit them and photographed them, costumed them and arranged them in statuesque poses. Altogether he tended to isolate individual gestures rather than film a flow of movements which would have made more demands on the actors.

Certainly, there are actors like Marlon Brando and Jeanne Moreau whose flickerings of temperament are highly photogenic but generally the impact an actor makes in a film depends more on his face and less on his voice – less on the way he speaks his lines – than it does in the theatre. In a play, the action is fuelled entirely by words and however widely interpretations of a play or a part may vary, the rhythm must derive from the script. In a film, the sequence of images is far more important than the words spoken, and the film as we know it now has evolved directly out of the silent film. The story is told through action: any young child can make far more sense of an adult film than of an adult play. The role of the writer in the cinema is proportionately smaller. Robert Bolt has found that the only way to make sure that his screenplays are used more or less as written is by collaborating with the director in the actual writing. In forty odd years of sound films, not a single writer has made his name through films, though many have made their fortunes. It is only a tiny minority in a cinema audience that has any interest in knowing who has written the script.

In an article on John Huston, James Agee described the first shot of Edward G. Robinson in *Key Largo* as 'one of the most powerful and efficient "first entrances" of a character on record'.[1] Robinson is seen naked in a tub of cold water, chewing on a cigar. This is bold and effective, but it is misleading to compare it with a theatrical entrance. No technique at all is involved on the actor's part. Robinson is a very good actor but the impact of this particular moment could have been achieved by anyone else who looked like him – if there were anyone else who looked like him. In the theatre, this kind of effect could only be obtained by bringing the lights up on the actor in the tub at the beginning of a scene. The impact would be smaller because the image on the retina would be smaller and a play is obviously limited in the number of times it can begin a new scene, whereas the camera can move wherever it pleases and, without pausing for scene breaks, the director can string together any number of moments like this which create their effect visually.

In this way, an actor can be made to give the impression of acting when he is not acting at all. The classic proof of this is provided by an experiment Kulyeshov once made.[2] He took an expressionless still of the actor Mosjoukine and he intercut the same shot with shots of a soup-plate, a corpse and a woman. When he showed the film, spectators thought they had watched subtle expressions of hunger, grief and love on the actor's face.

There is an almost equal absence of acting in a great many films which involve a lot of violent action – gun-fights, fist-fights, car chases, riots, stampedes, fires, canoes crashing

---

[1] *James Agee on Film*, Peter Owen.
[2] It was cited by Raymond Durgnat in an article in *Films and Filming*, February 1965.

over rapids, cavalry charges, war dances. Any number of thrillers and Westerns have been produced in which situation and spectacle make the actual business of speaking lines so unimportant that any photogenic stunt man could give an adequate performance in a central part, provided only that he did not tense up in the presence of cameras.

Even in films which make greater demands on the actor's talents, the conditions of cinema do a lot to blur the distinction between a good actor and a bad actor. Sound recording is better today than it has ever been, but many cinemas have inferior loudspeakers, and however good the recording and however good the reproduction, it is bound to take quite a lot of the edge off vocal inflections and to deaden variations of tone.

Post-synchronization introduces another layer of artificiality. It is impossible to reproduce the same sounds sitting round a microphone in the recording studio that you made while you were moving about on location. Jean-Luc Godard has latterly taken to using synchronized sound in all his films, believing that the loss of clarity is preferable to making audiences watch one performance and listen to another.

In every way, though, the film actor is far less in control than the stage actor of the effect he is going to have on his audience. Quite apart from being unable to gear his performance to their reactions, his impact is dependent on a great many factors which he cannot control and cannot easily gauge. A camera which is positioned some distance away may be filming in close-up. This is a matter of the focal length of the lens and the director is not going to stop to tell him what it is, but he is expected to sense more or less what sort of shot he is in and to scale his movements right down at the moments when half his face is going to fill the whole screen. Usually, in fact, he can guess when he is being shot in close-up. As in stage work, technical knowledge needs to be assimilated so deeply that it operates almost instinctually. It is fatal to be distracted by calculating how to angle the chin or bend an elbow but it is important to be roughly aware of how things are going to look on the screen.

But however he plays a line or a reaction, its impact on the audience is largely dependent on how much of him they see, at what distance, at what angle, what else is in frame, the lighting and the sound track. The actor never knows whether background music is going to be introduced, and audiences are so conditioned to it that they are not always aware that it is played and hardly ever remember afterwards. But instead of leaving it to the actor to create the mood, the music takes over. There is a scene in Hitchcock's *Psycho* for instance when Janet Leigh, playing a secretary who has just stolen a large sum of money, drives a car along a road. It is a very exciting scene but the excitement does not derive from anything Janet Leigh is doing. It comes partly from the situation – the money is with her in the car – but mainly from Bernard Herrmann's background music. As Herrmann pointed out in a television interview, the music was designed to create suspense by hinting that something unpleasant was likely to happen at any moment to the pretty secretary.

There is a great deal the actor cannot control but the demands on his self-control and concentration are enormous. Dialogue is often rewritten during filming and an actor may only get a new scene on the day he has to shoot it. He never knows when he is going to be called and there are long periods of waiting about followed by long periods of intensive work shooting the same sequence over and over again. If it is an emotionally demanding scene, it is easy to get tired and impatient and to feel that each retake is worse than the last. Often it is. And although most directors would agree in principle with Renoir, who said[1] that he wanted the movements of the camera to be determined by the actors, not the movements of the actors by the camera, it is often necessary to make the actor work in cramped and unnatural positions or at unnatural angles in relation to his partner in the scene. He

[1] *Sight and Sound*. Winter 1958–9.

may have to play part of a love scene to an imaginary point three inches to the left of the camera while the actress is in her dressing-room and the cues are being read from a script by someone standing to the right of the camera. He may have to shoot several successive takes of a quarrel on a staircase, speaking the same lines on the same stairs each time, leaning at the same angle over the same point of the banister, and placing his reactions, as well as timing them in the same way in each retake. He may have to play a scene with another actor which involves changing the angle of the relationship to him at each cut, perhaps turning away from him at the moment when he most needs to look him in the eye. In repeating takes, any but the smallest variation in movement is liable to be difficult for the cameraman to follow: even a new gesture of the hands can take them out of picture or bring them into it when only the face is wanted. He also has to contend with the distractions of the make-up girl who hurries in to powder his forehead and comb his hair between each take, while the director is maybe briefing him. And he has to work all the time in the centre of a small crowd of assistant-directors, electricians, props men, stand-ins and extras.

Working in a studio, there is less atmospheric help to be had from the set than there is in the theatre, where there is no light on anything else. Under the batteries of powerful lights in a film studio, everything else is lit up too and even though the set itself may be more realistic, it is liable to be broken up into component pieces which are rearranged in different combinations and at different angles. Out of doors, of course, the gain in realism is enormous, and it is not just a matter of having a real mountain, a real mill, a real fire, a real avalanche, a real crowd throwing stones. Actors respond to a new physical environment and the distractions of the open air – rain and bird-cries and the sound of waves – can in fact be a help to concentration.

On location or in the studio, all the props are more realistic than in the theatre. Discussing *Saturday Night and Sunday*

Morning on television, Albert Finney said how exciting he found it to work on a real lathe in the Raleigh factory.

> When I was being photographed working at that lathe, then I could absolutely concentrate on what the character was supposed to do. There was no cheating involved, you know. On the stage it would have been made of cardboard, and part of my job as an actor would have been convincing the audience that the cardboard lathe was a real one.

One of the biggest differences of all in filming is that instead of having a rehearsal period of several weeks in which no one needs to give a performance, few films have any rehearsal at all, except for running through each sequence immediately before it is shot. Scenes are taken out of order, breaking them down into short sections – sometimes only three or four lines at a time. So instead of having a whole rehearsal period of maybe ten weeks in which to find his character by working on his own and with the others at rehearsals, the actor has to commit himself to a characterization on his first day. Whatever he uses by way of accent, mannerisms, stance, gait, rhythms of speaking and gesturing, make-up and hair-style, he must stick to throughout the next days or weeks or months of filming, concentrating not only on the character's overall consistency but on his development from scene to scene. One sequence which follows chronologically after another may be shot weeks later, and while it is up to the continuity girl to take careful note of which shoes he should be wearing and whether his sports jacket is buttoned or not and whether the pocket flaps are in or out, she cannot help with the sequence of moods. It is up to the actor himself not to come into the house with a broad smile if he walked up the drive seven weeks ago in a deep depression. Or if he does, to make the change of mood mean something to the audience.

And whereas part of the technique of acting in the theatre lies in repeating a performance night after night and making every part of it look spontaneous, the film actor never does any repeating, except the immediate repetition of one take after another. So theoretically, he never needs to play a scene well more than once, assuming that the other actors and the technicians are equally satisfactory in the same take. Some film actors boast that there is only one good take in them; stage actors would think this was something to be ashamed of. But many things which happen spontaneously, and many things which are unrepeatable, find their way into films. This is why amateurs, children, animals, accidents and incompetent blondes, which can all be disastrous in the theatre, can be put to good use in films. Hugh Griffith was not acting when he pulled his horse over on top of him as Squire Western in *Tom Jones* but the cameras were on him and the incident is very funny in the finished film. Pudovkin has described how he once found he could only get the gratified smile he needed from a boy, a bad actor, by telling him what a good actor he was, and once, to get the expression he wanted from Lauren Bacall, John Huston twisted her arm.

The performance never exists as a whole, except on celluloid, and even there, the audience may never see more than thirty uninterrupted seconds of any single performance as the film cuts from one actor to another. In the theatre he can think his way logically and chronologically through the character's development but in filming he plays each sequence separately and without having played the sequence that leads into it. Actors who film parts they have previously played in the theatre invariably find that the knowledge they already possess is a big help in dotting backwards and forwards over the character's development but in most cases the film actor never gets a run on the whole part. He may never even read it as a whole.

In his book *Film Acting* (1933) Pudovkin was highly critical of this aspect of film-making practice. He had himself suffered as an actor at the hands of directors who gave instructions like jut out the chin, open the eyes wide, bend or raise the head – without allowing him time to make sense of what he was having to do. But above all he hated the discontinuity of the work, maintaining that the actor would never be able to give of his best unless it were made possible for him to feel that the 'separate pieces of his role' were all within his control. In order to establish 'the inner unity of any given piece with the role as a whole', Pudovkin suggested that actors should be rehearsed in the same way that they are in the theatre. Special scripts would have to be prepared, incorporating all the separate sequences and replacing any episodes that would be hard to rehearse (like swimming across a river) with simpler alternatives which would serve the same function in the story. The director would then revise the shooting script in the light of what he had learned from rehearsals, and, during the shooting, he would take time to explain the reasons for each movement of the camera.

> The film actor must feel the urge and the necessity for a given camera position for the shooting of any given piece of his role in precisely the same way as a stage actor feels the necessity, at a given point in the course of his role, for making an especially emphasized gesture, or for advancing to the footlights, or for ascending two steps of a scenery stair.

Finally, the actors would be invited to collaborate in the cutting. Needless to say, these ideas were never put into practice, and the actor's needs and feelings still come fairly low in the hierarchy of priorities. As Alain Resnais has said,[1] 'How rarely we alter the shooting to suit an actor's feelings, whereas we are always altering it to suit the weather.'

Actors vary in their reactions to the conditions of filming. Some are glad to avoid direct contact with an audience and there are few who are not glad to avoid long runs. Some welcome the close participation of the director in the actual performance but I have yet to meet one who likes the fact that his performance can be substantially altered after he has

[1] In an interview in *Films and Filming*, February 1962.

finished working on it. Very few people outside films realize how much can be done by the editor in the cutting room. By piecing together bits from different takes of the same sequence the editor can create something very different from what the actor actually did, and sometimes the performance emerges as distinctly better. Anyone seeing the rushes of *The Prince and the Showgirl* could have had serious doubts about Marilyn Monroe but Jack Harris rendered her a service which he afterwards called 'love-cutting'.[1]

It is often the editor who determines the timing of pauses and reactions. Pauses can be lengthened or shortened both on the screen and on the soundtrack. In the country walk scene in *Accident*, so far as the audience is concerned, it is Dirk Bogarde as Stephen who determines how long his hand lingers on top of the gate next to Anna's, but in fact it is always the editor who decides whether to accept or alter the actor's timing. However good his instinct is, the actor is never in a position to finalize the length of a pause because he never knows exactly what is going to be on the screen. The length of the pause must depend on whether he is on camera himself all through the pause, and in what sort of shot, and whether (and when) the camera cuts to someone else's reaction or to a close-up of a detail (like the hands on the gate). So the rhythm and tempo of a film are effectively determined in the cutting room.

A whole new scene can be created there, too, as Sir John Gielgud has described in an interview.

Somebody told me the other day that in Orson Welles's film *The Chimes at Midnight*, in which I play Henry IV, one of the most effective moments is one after Hotspur's death in which I look at Falstaff, at Hotspur's body, and then at Prince Hal; but we never did the scene at all. On the last day Orson said, 'There's a close-up I have to do

[1] *Sight and Sound*, Spring 1966. James Clark in an interview with Roger Hudson.

of you, just look down there, that's Hotspur's body, now look up at me.' I never even saw Orson made up as Falstaff, but it appears that, because of the clever cutting, this scene of glances between four people is enormously effective.[1]

If the editor and the director both have so much power over an actor in film, can we say that a whole performance can be put together like this? It could be argued that what von Sternberg did for Marlene Dietrich in *The Blue Angel* was to edit her. He cut out the movements and mannerisms that he did not want, cleverly dressing up the elements he did want and pasted the bits together, superimposing them on a contrived background to produce an effect which was far beyond the reach of the actress. Dietrich was a good pupil and not completely inexperienced. She had done some work on the stage and made a few films but acquired very little confidence in herself as a film actress. Emil Jannings, on the other hand, who plays the gauche, provincial, authoritarian schoolmaster, had played leading parts for Reinhardt and starred in several films – most notably as the cloakroom attendant in Murnau's *The Last Laugh*. He was generally considered to be one of the greatest living actors, but Dietrich, who seems to be doing next to nothing, makes his performance look bombastic, mannered and superficial.

Like so many film stars, she conveys strong contradictory impressions of immediacy and remoteness, availability and elusiveness. In his book *From Caligari to Hitler*, Dr Siegfried Kracauer has called Lola-Lola

a new incarnation of sex. This petty bourgeois Berlin tart with her provocative legs and easy manner, showed an impassivity which incited one to grope for the secret behind her callous egoism and cool insolence. That such a secret existed was also intimated by her veiled voice which, when she sang about her interest in love-making and nothing else,

[1] *Great Acting*, BBC Publications.

vibrated with nostalgic reminiscences and smouldering hopes.

What was the secret? Perhaps the riddle posed by the one quotation can be solved by another, from Louise Brooks:

Dietrich always mystified me because I wondered 'What in hell is she thinking about – with that long gorgeous stare?' Sternberg solves the mystery in one simple line of direction. He used to say to her 'Count six and look at the lamp-post as if you couldn't live without it!' So by giving her these strange thoughts to concentrate on, to build her mind, he also of course gave her this strange, alien mystery. She never had it with any other director. . . . He could direct every woman he touched. He could make her lovely! He could take the most gauche, awkward specimen and turn her into a *dynamo* of sex! . . . . Sternberg could look at a woman and say, 'This is beautiful about her, I'll leave it, not change it. And this is ugly about her. I'll eliminate it. Not change her but take away the bad and leave what is beautiful so she is complete.'

For instance, Dietrich – if you ever saw her in those pre-von Sternberg films, she was just . . . dynamic! Full of energy and awkward. Just dreadful! . . . So he simply cut out her movements and painted her on the screen in beautiful, striking poses, staring at a lamp-post.[1]

Of course, Louise Brooks is not exactly an impartial witness for her own career suffered from the advent of talkies. After starring in a number of silent films for Pabst, including *Pandora's Box* and *The Loves of Jeanne Ney*, her reputation was rapidly eclipsed by Dietrich's. Dietrich had four very bad years from 1935 to 1939, when, after her seven films for von Sternberg, she started working with other directors – Borzage, Boleslavski, Feyder and Lubitsch. She made a big comeback

[1] Positif No. 75 May 1966 quoted by John Kobal in *Marlene Dietrich*. Studio Vista.

in *Destry Rides Again* (1939), a hilariously funny Western, in which, far from doing nothing, she kicked several men's bottoms, wrestled with Una Merkel and threw a prodigious quantity of china as a hot-tempered saloon-bar songstress. And since then her popularity has scarcely waned.

That she has a great talent is unquestionable. It is also fairly clear that though she developed a formidable technique afterwards, she was technically very raw at the time of *The Blue Angel*. But even if film stars can give highly effective performances without technical *savoir faire*, it does not follow that film actors do not need technique and it is also true that technique and concentration are involved in turning the face into a mask expressive of absolutely nothing. The famous last scene in *Queen Christina* started in a long shot of Garbo at the prow of the ship and dollied into a sustained close-up of her staring into the distance. The Queen has given up her kingdom to live with a lover who has just died in her arms after being wounded in a duel with her previous lover. Mamoulian directed her in the final shot by asking her to think of nothing. And it works – not because her face is expressive, though it can be, but because at this moment, it is not. It is like a beautiful mask and it is touching in the same way that a classical mask or a Noh mask can be. Emotion is aroused in the audience and projected on to it in such a way that the mask itself seems to be doing something to produce the emotion.

There is a very striking example of the way this can happen in *The Jazz Singer* (1927). This is a thoroughly bad film with one excellent scene in it as Al Jolson is putting on his black make-up in the middle of an emotional scene with the girl who loves him (May McAvoy). He was not a good actor and he did not have a good face but the black has the effect of almost rubbing his features out and it is very strange to watch it going on. When the make-up is completed by the addition of a short-haired frizzy wig, he is momentarily tragic. He only has to hang his head sadly for the effect to be very moving.

When Salvini was an old man, he was asked how he could still manage to shout so vigorously in the theatre. His reply was 'I do not shout. You do the shouting for me'.[1] In the cinema, it is the audience that does a lot of the acting.

///

10 · STYLES OF FILM ACTING

Eisenstein started his professional life as a designer in the theatre and when he was working on *The Mexican*, a play adapted from a Jack London short story, he wanted to build a boxing ring in the centre of the auditorium so as to approximate as closely as possible to the conditions of an actual boxing match. Like so many good ideas, this one was strangled in its cradle by fire regulations and the fight was enacted in a realistic boxing ring on the stage, though it was not scripted to take place in view of the audience at all.

> Our scene employed realistic, even textural means – real fighting, bodies crashing to the ring floor, panting, the shine of sweat on torsos and finally the unforgettable smacking of gloves against taut skin and strained muscles.[2]

Later, the idea of producing a play about a gas factory in a gas factory was tempting but unrealizable. But the factory had such 'plastic charm' that the play was dropped and they made a film about it instead.

Already in the incident of the boxing ring, there is a hint that Eisenstein's talents might be more cinematic than theatrical. The action of a boxing match has little to do with acting and the writer who dramatized the story was adhering

[1] Quoted in Stanislavski, *Building a Character*. Max Reinhardt.
[2] From an article by Eisenstein published in *Sight and Sound*.

more to the tradition derived from Greek tragedy in which all the violent action takes place off stage. But cinema is forced into a different kind of relationship with reality by its dependence on the camera, which is in its element when recording actual events. And violence is particularly photogenic. The camera always seems to be telling the truth and realistic studio sets and natural outdoor settings help the illusion. If it is a real prairie and a real mustang, the villain's death throes must be real too. The audience is not so aware that it is watching a *performance*.

So how much room is there in the cinema for acting? None at all, according to some critics. '*Actor*,' says David Thomson in his interesting book *Movie Man*, 'isn't even a term appropriate to the cinema. The barrier of the screen certainly gives the impression of acting but what we're seeing in the cinema is people . . . The requirement of cinema is not that a person should perform but that he should be observed, that events should be allowed to happen, rather than be designed.'[1]

There are many directors who think it easier to obviate the dangers of the wrong sort of performance by using amateur actors. Bresson, the most important of these directors, has a very low opinion indeed of professionals. This is what he said about them to Jean-Luc Godard in an interview published in *Cahiers du Cinéma*:

L'acteur ne s'arrêtera jamais de jouer, premièrement. Le jeu, c'est une projection – votre personnage non-acteur doit être absolument fermé, comme un vase avec un couvercle. Et ça, l'acteur ne peut pas le faire, ou, s'il le fait, à ce moment là, il n'est plus rien . . . quand l'acteur se simplifie, il est encore plus faux que quand il joue . . . Nous sommes complexes, et ce que projette l'acteur n'est pas complexe . . . la plupart des films (et c'est aussi pour cela qu'il m'est si désagréable d'aller au cinéma) me paraissent des concours de grimaces . . . cette espèce de

[1] David Thomson, *Movie Man*. Secker & Warburg.

mimique perpetuelle – et la voix, en plus ce ton qui donne une voix absolument fausse . . . la mécanique est la seule chose, comme au piano. C'est en faisant des gammes, et c'est en jouant de la façon la plus regulière et la plus mécanique qu'on attrape l'émotion. Ce n'est pas en cherchant à plaquer une émotion comme font les virtuoses.

According to Bresson, 'Films can only be made by by-passing the will of those who appear in them, using not what they do but what they are.' He used well-known actors in his earlier films but now he prefers to voyage with his camera over unexplored acting territories, never knowing quite where he is going to end up. In casting Claude Laydu to play the lead in *Le Journal d'un Curé de Campagne*, Bresson found an inexperienced young actor with a very expressive face and the ability to respond fruitfully to instructions, discovering fresh depths in his own personality as he went through the experiences of Bernanos's suffering priest. Bresson has not always been as fortunate in his leading men (*Pickpocket, Un Condamné à Mort s'est échappé*) but returning to one of Bernanos's doomed villages in *Mouchette*, he gets an unforgettable performance out of Nadine Nortier as the fourteen-year-old girl. After being raped by a poacher, she is driven to suicide, not as a direct result of the rape but because she gets totally isolated in a village society made up of schoolgirls who conform where she cannot, schoolboys who want her to watch while they drop their trousers and adults who are not interested in her unless they can use her.

Bresson is an extreme case but he is not by any means alone in wanting to by-pass the will of the actor. It is for the same reason that so many Italian neo-realist directors used amateurs.

Of course it must not be taken as axiomatic that amateurs are totally lacking in technique. There is a technique in relaxing sufficiently in front of the cameras not to seem phoney and it is even more vital than it is in the theatre not to force the face muscles into registering a desired expression. This is the mistake Jannings makes in *The Blue Angel*. It is far too obvious that he is willing himself into a demonstration of blustering anger or affronted dignity or passionate desire or pathetic humiliation. He knows exactly the effect he wants and, too transparently, goes right out to get it. In 1929, while Expressionism was encouraging a fairly rhetorical style of acting in the German theatre, Jannings's performance would not have stuck so badly in the throats of cinema audiences, but today our preference for underplaying is so deep-seated that it looks inferior to the performances of Claude Laydu or Nadine Nortier or the amateurs who played the father and son in *Bicycle Thief* – Lamberto Maggiorani and Enzo Staiola.

For the director who gains the confidence of his amateurs, it is not difficult to teach them most of the technique they need as they go along. De Sica has described his methods of working with amateurs in an interview:

> In many ways they are more flexible and more intensive in their reactions than professional actors. At first of course, when they feel the eye of the camera fixed on them, they become very self-conscious, stiff and absurdly awkward. They can't even sit down without upsetting the chair. My method to get them back to their natural selves is simply to live with them for days, even for weeks on end, until they treat me as a friend and forget all about 'acting'. My experience as an actor helps me enormously to time the take and to catch them just at the right moment.[1]

And certainly he got excellent results from amateurs. Maria Pia Casilio, who gave a very pleasing performance as the maid in *Umberto D*, subsequently became a professional actress but she never made any comparable impact.

All this may seem to add up to saying that directors can give actors all the training and experience they need in the

[1] *Sight and Sound*, April 1950.

process of shooting, but this is only true of certain kinds of film. The 'neo-realistic' films in which de Sica and Visconti used amateurs were part of a post-war wave of concern with immediate social realities, and both directors reverted to using professionals when they turned to films which centred more on personal relationships – de Sica with *Stazione Termini* (1953) and Visconti with *Bellissima* (1952) and *Senso* (1954).

Since *Les Dames du Bois de Boulogne* (1944–5), Bresson has used very few professionals but it is no accident that in his two best films, *Le Journal d'un Curé de Campagne* (1951) and *Mouchette* (1966), both protagonists are chiefly passive. The priest, like the girl, is a defenceless innocent in an unsympathetic landscape populated entirely by depraved and hardened egocentrics. In fact the situation of both characters is paradigmatically illustrated by the opening shots of *Mouchette*, which set the tone for the whole film. We see a bird getting caught in a noose and then flailing about in growing panic as its attempts to escape only make the noose go tighter. Like the scene of the epileptic fit, with the child wiping blood and saliva from the poacher's mouth, or like Eisenstein's boxing match, the sequence makes a strong visual impact, but it has nothing to do with acting.

While David Thomson's remarks are perfectly valid for films like this, most of the important films in the history of the cinema lean quite heavily on performances which could only have come from highly skilled professionals. What would the cinema be without Keaton and Chaplin, Raimu and Michel Simon, Cagney and Bogart, Bette Davis, Orson Welles, Olivier, Brando, Toshiru Mifune, Magnani, Moreau and Belmondo?

Raymond Durgnat[1] has divided the different styles of acting in the history of the film into eleven categories: (1) the '*semaphore*' of stylized gestures and signals in the early silent films; (2) the *pantomime* style of Mack Sennett; (3) the

[1] *Films and Filming*, February 1965.

Expressionism of the Golden Age of German silent films; (4) the early style of Eisenstein and Pudovkin with brief shots of fixed expressions; (5) the later silent style, accepted then as realistic; (6) the modification of this into the 'mainstream' sound style; (7) the 'monumental' style of Dreyer's *The Passion of Joan of Arc* and *Ivan the Terrible*; (8) the swift fluid responsiveness of Renoir's Thirties films; (9) the blend of (7) and (8) in early Antonioni and Visconti films; (10) the understatement of English war films and (11) *cinéma vérité*. Useful though this is as a thumbnail history of the cinema, it seems odd that only five of his eleven categories should relate to the forty years since sound came in. (Or six categories if we include *cinéma vérité* which has nothing in itself to do with acting but has had an effect on it in encouraging ever more realistic underplaying.) Despite an overwhelming majority of bad films, the last forty years have yielded rich crops of possibilities, few of which have been harvested yet. Cinema has altogether had only a very short history, compared with the theatre, but though it is basically a medium which demands a greater realism, it is interesting that, just as in the theatre, each new wave of acting has aimed at being more realistic than the last.

In the silent films, of course, it was hard to achieve much realism. The comedy of Mack Sennett's Keystone Cops lent itself ideally to violent gestures and exaggerated facial expressions, but the serious films tried to be realistic, however heavily the dice were weighted against them. The dialogue was usually written after the shooting was finished and Josef von Sternberg[1] tells the story of an actor who, on the silent stage, said 'Come on baby, let's beat it' only to find out when he saw the finished film that, according to the title, what he was saying was 'Darling, without you life has no meaning, please don't leave me.' And when John Ford[2] was asked by

[1] Sternberg, *Fun in a Chinese Laundry*. Secker and Warburg.
[2] An interview recorded in 1966: *John Ford* by Peter Bogdanovich. Studio Vista.

an interviewer whether he used to rehearse his actors in the silent days, the answer was

> You didn't have time for that. All you could tell an actor was where to move and you could speak to him during the scene – which was a great help. I wish we could now. Sometimes a woman would like a little music – thought it would help her – so I had Danny Borzage play his accordion softly.

One of the greatest difficulties was getting actors to show emotion without putting on a demonstration. Griffith's *Birth of a Nation* (1915) has extras literally jumping for joy at the baptism of the Confederacy flag. Later, during a pause in trench fighting, the hero, Colonel Ben Cameron (Henry B. Walthall) takes out the photograph of the heroine (Lillian Gish) and shows his emotion by shaking his head. When he is lying wounded in hospital, she of course turns up as a nurse and she emotes with stiff arms and outspread hands, her mouth moving as if singing. Mae Marsh, as the Colonel's sister, is equally convulsive, with incessant hand movements, endearingly kittenish though they are. She signals joy with a lot of little jumps, and hand-claps come like punctuation. Her eyes flit round, darting everywhere, except into the camera. But she is much more convincing than Henry B. Walthall is at the big moment of his return home. She waits tremulously on the doorstep and when he appears, she launches herself to greet him with a huge hug. He merely looks embarrassed.

A lot of the comedy, though, has not dated at all. When Lincoln signs the order for her son to be released from hospital, Mrs Cameron is so happy that she very nearly throws her arms around her President. And there is a good comic sentry at the hospital who gazes longingly at Elsie (Lillian Gish). She is only two feet away from him but she does not notice him. When she finally sees the hunger in his eyes, she takes two paces back.

Twelve years later when von Sternberg made *Underworld*, the problem was still the same. There is a great deal about George Bancroft's performance as the gangster Bull Weed which is very good, but his smiles and laughs seem outrageously exaggerated, especially when he reads the newspaper article saying that the police are closing in on the robbers, and he gives a great leer into the camera as he leaves his hideaway. As the little lawyer who is later going to fall in love with Bull Weed's girl, Clive Brook purses his lips to make himself look inappropriately prissy on the line which appears in the titles as 'I'm not interested in women'.

Douglas Fairbanks's silent films stand up better because he made capital out of the fact that realism was impossible. Every move is a swagger, every moment of stillness is a pose, every other exit is a vault and every smile is a great flash of the teeth. In *The Gaucho* (1928) a cigarette pokes arrogantly from the centre of his mouth all through the film, even when he is beating a man up or receiving his guests at a supper party. But there is a humorous relish in the way he twirls it to the side of his mouth to kiss a girl he is dancing with. (The fact that her body is lassoed to his is typical.) The cigarette falls from his lips only when the vengeful victim of the Black Doom reaches through an open window to clasp his hand, deliberately infecting him with the disease.

The titles are sentimentally humourless. 'You're like one night on the pampas . . . I was alone . . . A full moon rose . . . A bird sang.' But Fairbanks's swashbuckling movements have an amazing self-awareness about them as he shows his athletic prowess, somersaulting into the saddle, or mounting with a girl in his arms, or once, aided no doubt by trick photography, walking almost vertically up the trunk of a tree in an escape sequence, and then doing a series of Tarzan swings from one tree to another, ending with a gigantic leap, carrying a tree-top with him like part of a giant catapult, to land safely on the ground.

The girl, Lupe Velez, had developed a pleasant technique

of breathing rapidly to make her bosom quiver whenever jealous, angry or amorous. Fairbanks's self-satisfaction lifts his movements on a tide of exuberance almost into the realm of ballet, but it does not save him from over-demonstrative movements, like the mammoth shrug of despair when he tries to dig his way out of prison with his bare hands and has to give up when he reaches the bedrock. But his cheerful, gutsy attack carries the film briskly and enjoyably forward.

The early talkies, using a mixture of silent screen actors and stage actors, suffered from much the same heaviness of touch as the serious silent films. Cagney, who had been a female impersonator and worked in vaudeville, was later to develop a very smooth screen technique but in his early films, like *Public Enemy* (1931), it is hard not to be aware of an uneasy application of stage principles – contriving for instance to show his head at a better angle by turning to talk to someone out of view to the right of the camera.

Many of the silent stars failed to survive into the talkies. John Gilbert was the most famous casualty. He had signed a million dollar contract just before sound came in and films were actually made which, because of his thin, high pitched voice, were never distributed. Thanks to Garbo, who resisted the pressure to make her accept Olivier as her leading man, Gilbert was used in *Queen Christina* but Mamoulian says he had to keep reminding him between each take to keep his voice down.

Within one decade, the Thirties, a style of film acting was evolved which is still in existence today, though of course it is not the only one in existence. But if we compare John Ford's *The Iron Horse* (1924) with his *Stagecoach* (1939) we see how much was achieved by Hollywood actors in the Thirties, however rubbishy the bulk of the material on which they had to cut their teeth.

So far as the acting is concerned, *The Iron Horse* is typical of the serious silent films, with staring bulbous eyes operatically signalling fear, and one actor (J. Farrell McDonald as

Corporal Casey) who busily semaphores every emotion with his bushy eyebrows. In *Stagecoach*, the acting is neither subtle nor sophisticated, but in comparison it seems both. Certainly it is as good as most of the film acting we are getting thirty years later, extracting every chance from a script (by Dudley Nichols) that provides plenty. The action moves, with the stagecoach, across the picturesque Arizona plains, and beside the tensions of strained relations between the passengers, there is the overall tension of danger from attacks by the Apaches – the soldiers who were due to escort the coach have not turned up. The action is at its most exciting when the Indians start their attack but the acting is more exciting before the attack, when the passengers characterize themselves by their reactions to the danger. Andy Devine gives a richly flavoured comic performance as the scared driver longing to turn back but too weak to resist the pressure put on him by the sheriff (George Bancroft again, much more effective when he can make himself heard).

Claire Trevor gives an admirably restrained performance as the good-natured prostitute who has been run out of town. Except for Ringo (John Wayne) who is on his way to prison in the sheriff's custody, all the passengers ignore her and insult her until she proves herself selfless, brave and invaluable in helping the drunken Doc Boone when Lucy Mallory gives birth to her child at a farm where they spend the night. Thomas Mitchell enjoys himself very enjoyably as the doctor, coaxing more and more samples out of the timid whisky salesman (Donald Meek) and then making a ferocious effort to sober up under a cold water tap. John Carradine lends a stubborn misplaced chivalry to the gambler Hatfield, who falls in love with Mrs Mallory (who certainly does not look pregnant) and goes on the journey specially in order to protect her. Berton Churchill adds his portly presence as an embezzling bank manager who puffs up pompously as he hectors the others and John Wayne does not need to do very much as the prisoner who quietly defends the prostitute. But he makes the most of the wooing scene, faltering shyly as he tells her about his farm across the border, and he manages to put together enough evidence of strength to make the ending almost credible. Getting parole from the sheriff, he fights a gun duel with three men and then returns triumphantly to be driven off to prison.

None of the casting is against type but of these central performances only Claire Trevor's, Louise Platt's (as Lucy Mallory), John Wayne's and George Bancroft's could be called straight. The character performances are all effective, all well-judged, all (except Thomas Mitchell's) underplayed, and they all match in very well with the straight performances. Even with Thomas Mitchell there is not the slightest feeling of a clash of styles. Claire Trevor is alone though in suggesting that the character has anything of an inner life. With a depth and a subtlety that go far beyond the script, she makes the audience participate in the girl's inarticulate helplessness in a situation she has created for herself without knowing what she was doing, and without having much choice anyway. The other performances all succeed in suggesting the lives that the characters lead, but without inviting us to see beyond them, as we need to if we are to put them in perspective. But then if it were not for Claire Trevor's giving so much more than the film demands, we would not dream of expecting anyone else to do more than they do. It is not by any means a Brechtian performance but it is both more and less than a wholehearted impersonation.

Stagecoach is an exceptionally good specimen of an unexceptional type. It is a Western with a straight narrative line, but it depends, as the vast majority of films do, largely on tensions created inside the confines of story-line and situation, by clashes of personality. It depends, therefore on actors to present the personalities and control the clashes. No director could make a film like this with amateurs.

A very different American film, made only a year later but much more modern, is *Citizen Kane*. This makes enormous demands on the actors who have to play their characters at a variety of different ages. Though the shooting did not necessarily jump them backwards and forwards in time as the finished film does, they still had to find the rhythms, the feelings, the movements and the voices to go with the different make-ups.

The changes in appearance are staggeringly effective. Welles's forehead seems to grow taller and older, and his acting – as opposed to his talent in directing the film – has not been praised anything like enough. He was only twenty-four and he transforms himself from the attractive young man, striding with loose-limbed, moneyed confidence around the office of the newspaper he is taking over into an even more confident politician and, when his public career suddenly capsizes, he slides rapidly into middle-age. He goes through over a dozen changes of make-up and his build and weight seem to vary as much as his voice. He swells to his fullest resonance in his brief political phase, narrowing and hardening vocally after his defeat, as he ages rapidly, and gets lonelier, and madder. The crucial change comes when he loses his wife, Susan. She cannot bear the force of his enormous will-power which works on her life like a battering-ram, driving her into the operatic career she does not really want, and when she walks out on him, we look on as he actually turns the corner into middle-age. The spine stiffens, the walk loses its springiness as he lumbers along the corridor to her empty bedroom. Then, with great technical prowess, he preserves the stiffness through awkward violent actions like throwing her suitcases about and finally, smashing up her bedroom.

As Susan, Dorothy Comingore, too, deteriorates remarkably. In the scene where the journalist interviews her in the empty nightclub, it is partly the lighting and the wig which give the impression that her face has got so much fatter, but the gin is audible in her voice. George Coulouris, as Thatcher, the lawyer, seems to get heavier and more solemn as his hair recedes and Everett Sloane, as Bernstein, the clerk, has to contend with almost as many changes of age, wig and make-up as Welles himself. His voices are all so convincing I wondered whether some of them were dubbed. The only actor who could not quite cope with the age-changes was Joseph Cotten, whose face does not take make-up at all well. As an old man he had to be shot in a peaked cap and a moustache, wearing sun-glasses for most of the scene and his age-cracked voice was nothing like so realistic as Everett Sloane's. He perhaps should have been dubbed.

It was at about this time that a distinctive English style in film acting emerged. In war-time the first duty of a movie camera is to make newsreels. While news was becoming more of a factor in national life than ever before, the documentary movement which had started in the Twenties came into its own. Semi-fictional documentaries like *Target for Tonight* (1941) were made to give the public a picture of what an air-raid was like from the viewpoint of the bomber crew. The parts were played by airmen and in Humphrey Jennings's *Fires Were Started*, a film about the incendiary raids on London, the actors were firemen. As the tendency towards merging fact and fiction together was gathering momentum, Noel Coward made his first film, *In Which We Serve*, scripting it, directing and playing the captain of a destroyer. Celia Johnson plays his wife, John Mills is a rating, Bernard Miles a petty officer and Richard Attenborough a young sailor who panics during a naval engagement. All five performances are intensely English, heroically throwing away lines with a self-regarding determination to be the opposite of self-regarding. At a time when sentimentality and patriotism were indistinguishable, it could not fail to have immense audience appeal, and it was to stay with us as a style for a good ten years after the war. Something of it still survives.

In 1944, Carol Reed's *The Way Ahead* did for the Army what Coward had done for the Navy. David Niven's performance in it, like Leslie Howard's in *The First of the Few* (as R. J. Mitchell, designer of the Spitfire), personified the combination of toughness and mildness which was basic to the style and to the idea of heroism it reflected. The hero was classic officer material, urbane, unflappable, reserved, full of generous emotion and romantic instincts held in behind a shell of perfect manners. And brave, of course.

It was the revolution which started in the theatre at the time of *Look Back in Anger* that turned the tide against this kind of hero and against this acting style. The new young actors like Albert Finney, Nicol Williamson, Peter O'Toole, Tom Courtenay, Alan Bates and Richard Harris were there, trained, ready (more or less) and waiting to be used, and suddenly realism meant regional accents. The English gentleman was dethroned. It is interesting to measure the extent of the reaction against the officer-hero type of acting by looking at *King and Country* (1964). The story, taken from James Lansdale Hodson's story *Hamp*, is set in the First World War, in the trenches. The dirt in the earlier war films was slightly romantic. Grime on the hero's face always looked good. In *King and Country*, much of the tone and atmosphere are set by totally realistic, totally unromantic mud, and by rats. The hero is a working-class soldier (Tom Courtenay) who has run away from the fighting and is now being court-martialled for desertion. The officers are all either unsympathetic or ineffectual, cowardly because (with one exception) they dare not look under the surface of his apparent cowardice. The military hierarchy, which epitomizes a society, depends on playing the game according to the rules which Private Hamp has broken. The Colonel (Peter Copley) is cold and narrow-minded, the Medical Officer (Leo McKern) is a gruff, blustering old fool who refuses to face even the possibility of mental unbalance, the platoon commander (Barry Foster) represents the worst possible ex-public school combination of heartiness, good intentions, irresponsibility and ineffectuality, while the Captain (James Villiers) is suave and stupid. The only sympathetic officer (Dirk Bogarde) starts off by finding it a great bore having to defend the unlucky private and then gets more and more involved as he comes to know him, only to find that there is nothing he can do except get drunk, after the death sentence is passed, and put a bullet in the boy's mouth when the firing squad fails to finish him off.

What of the future? It is not only new techniques in film-making that must affect the technique of film-acting, but also the fact that audiences are becoming so much more expert at watching films and television. Story-telling on screen can only proceed at the rate the audience can take, and in the early silent films it was very slow. It is too early to predict the effect that multiple screen techniques will have, for they are still at a relatively primitive stage of development, but in changing our filmic concept of space, they will force us to redefine time in film terms. An action which starts on one screen can continue on another, a flash-back can be shown simultaneously with action in the present tense and enactment of fantasy in the future – all this must affect acting. What is already clear is that audiences today can digest film story information far more quickly than ever. They belong to what *Life* magazine has described as 'the generation raised on TV, conditioned by commercials to accept as commonplace the zoom shot, the jump cut, the freeze-frame. This generation responds to the shock effect of total immersion, multiple-screen, multi-track movies with the same personal involvement that their grandfathers felt in reading *The Adventures of Tom Sawyer*.'

This must lead to the evolution – which has already started – of a style in film acting which can afford to take short cuts. Just as stage acting no longer needs to accrete details natural-istically, so, in films and eventually in television, we can expect to see more of the stripping down which makes timing more important and biographical background less. This is already observable in the films Jean-Luc Godard was making between 1959 (*A Bout de Souffle*) and 1965 (*Pierrot le Fou*).

It is sometimes said of Godard that actors do not need to act in his films. But in reality the films are not immune from being disfigured – or even pushed off balance – by bad acting. The main weakness in *Le Mépris* is Michel Piccoli's performance as the husband. He is exactly the right physical type but he lacks the technique to make himself felt. The character is negative but the playing of it needs to be much more positive. In some of his latest films like *Made in U.S.A.* (1966) Godard is himself confused about the plot. Even in *Pierrot le Fou*, which starred Anna Karina together with Jean-Paul Belmondo, the background of gangs and gun-running is kept in a very blurry focus. Accustomed as audiences all are to Hollywood thrillers, it is quite possible for them to accept these elements in the story as *données*, without demanding a coherent explanation of them. And this is the way Godard and Karina work with the role of Marianne, the destructive, disaffected girl who does not know what she wants. Her character is full of anomalies and mysteries and compulsions which neither Marianne nor Karina understands (why should they?) but we get Marianne into a very clear focus, as we do a Pinter character, from the rhythm of her words and her silences, and her actions and her inaction, without needing to know any fictional facts about her background.

Pierrot le Fou is excellent in its combination of fixed story and improvisation. The garage scene is like the garage scene in *Bonnie and Clyde* in that it makes the violence every bit as charming as the hero and heroine are, inviting the audience to identify and so trapping them into the question 'What would you do if you were in their situation? What if you had no money to pay for the petrol that had just been pumped into your tank and a burly garage man were running out at you?' Karina then solves the problem with a Laurel and Hardy gag, pointing up in the air and when the man looks up, hitting him hard in the stomach.

For Marianne and Pierrot, violence is a game which is

bound to end in death, for they know that they are 'characters', which helps the audience to take them much as they take themselves – seriously and not seriously at the same time. When Marianne expresses contempt of men who drive cars in straight lines, Pierrot takes the car off the road across the beach and into the sea. Karina shows all the edginess of a girl who gets what she wants fairly easily and soon tiring of it, grows restless and predatory. Alternating between affection and destructive hostility, her timing is itself provocative. In the 'Bogart' part in *Made in U.S.A.*, she kills but fails to come over as dangerous – we do not believe in her as a killer – but in *Pierrot* more than in any of his other films, Godard touches the temperamental roots of the tension Karina can create on the screen and she does emerge as dangerous. In the scene with the dwarf when he has the revolver and she has the scissors, she first snips idly at the corners of her hair and then holds them like a dagger, looking quite capable of sticking them in his throat. She also looks very hard to resist when she challenges Pierrot to steal the car. 'Show you're a man.' Her personality, her talent and her technique are indistinguishable here.

There are several set pieces of acting in the film which contrast effectively with the free-wheeling semi-improvisational style of most of the playing. In the sequence where they tell stories to the tourists for money, she does a parody of silent film type acting and then, in the Vietnam sketch, she does cod Vietnamese to Belmondo's cod American. He also does an imitation of Michel Simon, talking philosophically about his novel with a hoarse voice and exaggerated mouthing. Raymond Devos contributes a brilliant comedy routine as the man on the pier who tells the story about the gramophone record. There is a hysteria underlying it – he wants to be told 'Vous êtes fou' but it is full of vaudeville exaggerations as he sings, grimaces, strokes his own hands, mimes breaking the record and chants 'Est-ce que vous m'aimiez?'

These set pieces of comedy stand out against the very casual treatment of the two songs, which could hardly be less like production numbers. Both Karina and Belmondo succeed beautifully in giving the impression of behaving just as they might behave if no one were watching – romping about with each other or fooling about by themselves. Their movements here are a happy extension of their normal personality-revealing movements and particularly in *Ma Ligne de Chance* they simply seem to be having fun. He walks up a tree stump, jumps off, spins her round in his arms. She gives in to the music and to her enjoyment of her own movements which seem more than ever just an extension of her beautiful body. The scene, like the whole film, is a serious soufflé. Like some of Beckett's work, it plays around with the possibilities of showing people playing around in a way that throws light on the basic ontological question: what do their lives really consist of?

Then again, in a grave moment, the camera challenges Karina herself, as well as Marianne. 'Tu ne me quitteras jamais?' Pierrot asks. 'Oui bien sûr.' The tone is matter-of-fact but the camera stays relentlessly on her after the words stop. She looks down, she looks sideways, she tries looking into the camera. Her eyes drop.

Belmondo is never examined quite in this way, but Pierrot is given attitudes to his own attitudes. There are enough layers to the characterization for this to happen. 'Ah quel terrible cinq heures du soir' says his voice on the soundtrack after he has betrayed Marianne to the men who are torturing him to find out where she is. He is genuinely desolate but he expresses his desolation in a conscious pose, lying prostrate on the railway track. The movement is quite separate from the 'voice over'. Then he deflates it by getting up. The mood is quite different from his despair after shooting Marianne. This is something that he cannot contain. He yells as he hurls himself like an object through the bushes. While he is painting his face blue, he is on the telephone, trying to get through to Paris. (This is effective in the way business often is, making him less deliberate about either action.) The final explosion as he blows himself up is, of course, visually spectacular, but it is far less memorable than the blind movements of his hands around his head, first tying the sticks of dynamite into position and then trying to extinguish the flame before it is too late. As in all the best moments of the film, improvised detail merges perfectly into planned story, and the camera seems to be there partly as a medium for the narrative, partly as a means of recording what Belmondo and Karina did when they were playing the parts. For this is intrinsically interesting and is frankly being presented for its own sake.

---

11 · CHARACTERIZATION IN FILM

How much can the film actor do by way of characterization? If the technique of acting for films consisted solely in relaxing in front of the cameras, the answer would be nothing at all, and David Thomson is one of those who are not very far from believing that this is the right answer. Speaking of Anna Karina in close-up, he says

There's less impression of the character being presented to us than of a meeting with a stranger in which one notices the physical actions of behaviour without having any idea what sort of character lies behind them. When we look at Anna Karina we see not an intended meaning but an alert personality. It follows that the most effective actors and actresses in the cinema are those who can achieve such a degree of external relaxation while being filmed that the camera records their nature without defining it.[1]

[1] *Movie Man.*

This is a fair enough account of the impression that Karina makes in her Godard films but it is not at all fair in its implications about how she arrives at making it. In *Pierrot* she is doing something quite different from what she did in the earlier films when Godard was aiming to portray her as she herself was. After playing with Irving in *Madame Sans-Gêne*, Ellen Terry is reported to have said 'It seemed to me some evenings as if I were watching Napoleon trying to imitate Henry Irving.' In *Une Femme est une Femme* (1961) and *Vivre sa Vie* (1962), the stripper and the apprentice prostitute are trying to imitate Anna Karina.

In *Une Femme est une Femme*, Godard cut out all the takes which he thought were the best, saying that Karina revealed more of herself as a woman when she was not working so well as an actress.[1] And he actually edits into the finished film a take in which Anna Karina (whose native language is Danish) corrects herself in the middle of a sentence. She is in close-up, saying that women who cry are beautiful. 'Moi je trouve *con* les femmes modernes qui essaient de limi . . . non, ça va . . . ça va pas? . . . ça va pas?' And the good take follows on immediately 'Moi je trouve *con* les femmes modernes qui veulent imiter les hommes.' The insecurity of the actress about the line and the language is merged into the aggressiveness of the character, which also derives from insecurity. And Godard takes a particular pleasure in filming her perched precariously on the border-line between acting and not acting.

In 1961 and 1962 she improvised most of her dialogue.[2] In later films, like *Pierrot*, her acting technique had improved vastly as a result of all the experience she had had under Godard's direction and she was able to speak dialogue he had written as if she were improvising it.

---

[1] Quoted by Tom Milne in an article in *Sight and Sound*, Autumn 1962.

[2] For a good deal of inside information derived from interviews with Godard, see Richard Roud, *Jean-Luc Godard*. Secker & Warburg, 1967. For critiques of the films, see *The Films of Jean-Luc Godard*. Studio Vista, 1967.

How conscious, though, ought the film actor to be about his characterization? Should he plan how he is going to filter his personality or should he rely on the lines, the costume and make-up, the situation, the director and the inspiration of the moment? Should he ask himself 'What is the character like?' or 'What are the character's objectives?'

According to Antonioni, it is better if he does not make any plans or ask himself any questions.

The film actor need not understand, but simply be . . . the film actor should work not on the psychological level but on the imaginative one. And the imagination reveals itself spontaneously. It has no intermediaries on which it can lean for support. It is not possible to have a real collaboration between actor and director. They work on two different levels. The director owes no explanations to the actor except those of a very general nature about the people in the film. It is dangerous to discuss details . . . The director must not compromise himself by revealing his intentions . . .

I prefer to get results by a hidden method; that is, to study in the actor certain of his innate qualities of whose existence he is himself unaware. One can almost trick the actor by demanding one thing and getting another . . . The actor is one of the elements in the image itself. A line spoken by the actor in profile doesn't have the same meaning as one given full face. A phrase addressed to the camera placed above the actor doesn't have the same meaning it would have if the camera were placed below him.

These few simple observations prove that it is the director – that is to say whoever composes the shot – who should decide the pose, gestures and movements of the actors.

The same principle holds for the intonation of the dialogue. The voice is a 'noise' which emerges with other noises in a rapport which only the director knows. It is therefore up to him to find the balance or unbalance of these sounds.[1]

When he was shooting his first film, *Cronaca di un Amore* (1950), in which he used long sequences, panning to follow the actors uninterruptedly, he used to keep his cameras on them after the scene was finished.

> I had the feeling that it wasn't right for me to abandon the actor at a time when, having just enacted an intensely dramatic scene, he was left alone by himself to face the after-effects of that scene and its traumatic moments . . . I did this because I felt the best way to capture their thoughts, their states of mind, was to follow them round physically with the camera.

In this way, by using his actors, as Godard did, after they had stopped acting, he could not fail to record spontaneous facial reactions. He afterwards abandoned this way of working, but Milos Forman has used it both in *Peter and Pavla* and *A Blonde in Love*.[2] He uses an amateur actor to play Peter's father and makes him improvise a long moralizing speech. When the unfortunate man runs out of words, the camera keeps turning and the effect is funny because, for the audience, it is the character who seems to be floundering. Similarly, in *A Blonde in Love*, there is a scene where three soldiers find that not much fun is to be had from local girls in the dance-hall. The boredom of the characters merges with the uncertainty of the actors about what to do next.

When *cinéma-vérité* methods are introduced like this into the studio it becomes very hard to define the frontier between what is acting and what is not. To what extent is Jeanne

---

[1] *Michelangelo Antonioni*, interview in *Film Culture*, Nos. 22–3.

[2] See Peter John Dyer's article 'Star-crossed in Prague' in *Sight and Sound*, Winter, 1965–6.

Moreau acting in Antonioni's *La Notte*? She has said that she was very unhappy making the film. Antonioni refused to take her into his confidence about what he was doing with her, deliberately merging the confusion of the actress into the performance. The method works because Moreau is playing a wife, Lidia, who does not understand her own behaviour, just as the husband, Giovanni, does not understand why he gives in to the nymphomaniac who assaults him in the hospital. At one point Lidia takes a taxi into the outskirts of the city and makes the driver stop by a field. She wanders aimlessly into it, admiring the scenery. When a group of boys troops into the field and two of them start fighting, she stops the fight, half unintentionally by murmuring a protest, which diverts their attention to her and she runs away when one of them, with blood on his face, walks up to her. Later, during the thunderstorm at the industrialist's party, when many of the guests in *Dolce Vita* style, jump into the swimming pool, Lidia without knowing why, is about to follow suit, when a young man stops her. She lets him take her for a drive and she lets him caress her, but stops him from kissing her. She knows she is no longer in love with Giovanni and though he thinks he is still in love with her, she proves he is not by reading him a love letter he once wrote to her in the bedroom one morning when she was still asleep. His reaction now is to ask who wrote it. When he tries to make love to her, almost by force, she at first resists him. Then we see her arm creep up round his back as the camera moves away into a long shot.

So is it right, when asking an actress to play a woman who does not understand her own actions, not to explain the character to her? Certainly Antonioni got very good results from Moreau, at the cost – or perhaps partly as a consequence – of making her unhappy. But this method of working is only possible when the actress is not required to characterize. She plays Lidia straight. But in *The Red Desert* Monica Vitti could only have succeeded in the part of the neurotic heroine if she had been able to characterize, while Richard Harris's performance as the engineer Corrado fails dismally because it is only too obvious that he does not know what is required of him. Unlike Lidia in *La Notte*, Corrado has definite aims. Disillusioned with the Italian industrial ethos, but believing things could be done differently, he wants to get some of the factory workers to sign up with him to go off and start a new factory in Patagonia. But Richard Harris, who is normally capable of showing all the requisite qualities of disenchantment, drive and leadership, remained wooden and apathetic because he did not understand his objectives.

The more initiative a character has to take, the more the actor needs to understand his drives – not to be psychoanalytically informed about them, but at least to be aware of what they are. In *Morgan*, David Mercer's adaptation of his own television play *A Suitable Case for Treatment*, Vanessa Redgrave had a fairly passive part, which could be played straight, so she could afford to put herself entirely in the hands of the director, Karel Reisz.

The lovely thing about *Morgan* was that for the first time I had a part in which I hadn't a whole load as a character – a whole load of principles, of motives, of fixed wants. I just responded to the situations I found myself in, reacted without any kind of pattern at all . . . The first thing Karel told me was to take each bit as it came. I started to say, now, how do I think of this, what does the character think about? He said: 'Just take each bit as it comes, we'll discover each bit as it comes, and finally it'll add up to something. Or it won't . . .' What upsets me about acting myself, or watching other people, is that again and again we fall into the mistake of the logic of cause and effect, which I don't think has any relation to holding a mirror up to life. We will keep trying to make a pattern, we're dying to make a pattern out of it: a complex pattern if we're good at it, maybe a very complex pattern. But what's interesting is that there isn't a pattern; it is not to look for a pattern at all, but to try and seize the odd moments and let them make up what they will. I'm more excited at this moment for somebody to ask me to do something, and for me to do it immediately and unquestioningly. Because I now think I shall discover more by doing what they ask me, immediately and unquestioningly and trustingly, than by working it all out and raising doubts and questions, into which will come all my inhibitions and doubts as an actress, as a person.[1]

To have 'a whole load' of principles, motives and fixed wants means shaping your characterization around your consciousness of them. To discard this and to hand the problem of pattern over to a director or to chance, you are handing yourself over as a personality to be used and it will be your basic personality, not your conscious characterization, which provides the continuity between what you do in one sequence and what you do in another. You will still be using technique in creating the odd moments, and the better your technique is, the more expressive they will be, but you do not worry about the meaning or direction of what you are expressing. You are concerned with nothing beyond this particular fragment of experience, this moment of reaction. You are a long way away from the arrows that all point in the same direction. But when they were working together on *Isadora*, in which she had to sustain an accent and a characterization, Karel Reisz must have made very different demands on her.

And for David Warner, who played Morgan, this freewheeling approach would not have worked. Morgan does a great many things that would have seemed totally out of character if he had played the part straight. He puts a skeleton in the bed of the wife, Leonie, who is in the process of divorcing him, he blows up his mother-in-law with a small

---

[1] Vanessa Redgrave in a television interview, reprinted in *The Listener*.

bomb, he terrifies a ticket collector in an underground station by his imitation of a gorilla, he puts on a knuckle-duster and pockets a revolver to visit Leonie's boy-friend in his art gallery, he burns a hammer and sickle in a thick-pile carpet and he kidnaps Leonie to take her camping in Wales. But David Warner does not fall into the trap of making the pattern simple. He roughens up his voice and he makes good use of the costume – the peaked cap, the dark glasses and the long fisherman's-knit sweater. The glasses and the clothes even seem to affect the way he moves. But instead of making Morgan predictably aggressive and conventionally mad, he goes for a pensive, suffering eccentricity, without being over-serious about it. The comedy, in fact, comes out all the better because of the controlled contradictions in the characterization. He oscillates most amusingly between dark brooding and manic impetuosity. David Warner is also capable of a crisp detachment from his character, whereas Vanessa Redgrave, so long as she acts on her own statement about putting herself unreservedly in the hands of a director, must abdicate from any independent critical function.

Certainly, though, characterization in film must differ hugely from characterization on the stage. Except in rare films like Kozintsev's *Hamlet*, in which there were three months of preliminary meetings between director and actors, followed by months of rehearsal, before the shooting started,[1] there is no time to find the character in rehearsal. How far ahead of shooting the actor receives a script usually depends partly on his standing and partly on the size of the part, but even if he gets a reasonable amount of time, there is a limit to what can be done without knowing what the director wants or how he will have to orient his characterization in relation to the other performances. And because he is so much more clearly visible in film than he is in the theatre, the radius of departure from his own appearance and personality is smaller. Even Sir Alec Guinness is less protean on films than

[1] Grigori Kozintsev, *Shakespeare, Time and Conscience*. Hill and Wang.

he is in the theatre, though not all that much less. Gully Jimson, the hero of *The Horse's Mouth*, a film Guinness adapted himself from Joyce Cary's novel, is much further removed from his basic self than Morgan is from David Warner's. Gully is a belligerent, middle-aged delinquent and Guinness shambles about with hunched shoulders, an untidy growth of beard, a hirsute blond fringe and a voice suggesting lungs that have breathed little but prison air.

The director who contrasts most strongly with Antonioni and Bresson is Ingmar Bergman. Bresson never uses an actor more than once and Antonioni tends not to, except with Monica Vitti. Bergman uses his actors again and again, casting them well against type and incidentally developing them in the process. Gunnar Björnstrand, Harriet Andersson, Bibi Andersson and Max von Sydow have proved themselves immensely versatile and developed greatly in technique since their early films. Björnstrand in particular is a virtuoso character actor. He is not as protean as Guinness – he can always be recognized easily enough – but he filters his personality so well that he makes totally different impressions. In *Waiting Women* (1952) he was the comic husband trying to keep his end up against Eva Dahlbeck's attacks while they were stuck in a lift. In *Sawdust and Tinsel* (1953) he was the pompous actor manager. In *Smiles of a Summer Night* (1955) he was the shy, fastidious lawyer Egerman and in *The Seventh Seal* (1957) he was the sturdy squire, Jons. Then in *Wild Strawberries* (also 1957) he played the cold ineffectual son of the old professor.

Nearly all Bergman's actors, like Bergman himself, work on the stage as well as in the cinema. As an example of an actor who works exclusively in films and sees himself as essentially a character actor, we could take Richard Attenborough. He said in an interview[1] that the further he retreated from himself, the better he performed. Preparing to play the sergeant major in *Guns at Batasi*, he spent hours in

[1] With Benedict Nightingale in *The Times*, 8th January, 1968.

his cellar learning to shout from his diaphragm, he practised pouring pints of beer straight down his throat and he experimented with his spine and his stance:

> I worked from the outside in. I didn't think I understood the man until I knew how he stood and how it felt to stand like that, and what he looked like.

But in *Séance on a Wet Afternoon* he approached the externals through the internals, working hard on his own to find the inside of the lonely man and only then going on to his mannerisms.

David Thomson, though he cannot deny that a lot of film acting is character acting, kicks violently against it, grossly undervaluing performances like Brando's in *On the Waterfront* and Olivier's in *The Entertainer*.

> At the moment technique becomes apparent, one realizes how condescending and cautious the performances are. The apparent wealth of detail in one of Brando's, or Olivier's, performances is delusory because it's aggregative. Nothing is allowed to contradict or even to lie oddly in relation to other things . . . (The performances) presuppose a tangible reality like a script rather than a willingness to see what the plastic reality will be.

Of course there has been a lot of bad acting in films of which these criticisms would be valid, but it is odd to pick Brando and Olivier as culprits. Brando never imposes a pattern on a part from outside. He goes at it quietly, finding his own rhythms in his lines, making everything seem like improvisation and winding himself up to uncoil violently in moments of passion or protestation or anger. Far from being condescending or cautious, Brando's acting is exciting because it seems so dangerous. There may be a framework of conscious preparation but he keeps it well hidden and he looks likely to burst at any minute through the walls of any situation that contains him. Like Olivier, he has a volcanic quality and he makes us feel that if he erupts, there is no knowing where the flood of lava will stop.

Olivier's Archie Rice was conceived in the theatre, but I thought that the performance, unlike the play as a whole, adapted very well to the screen. It was maddening to lose all the long speeches and some excellent moments like the breakdown over the 'two nuns' story. This got terribly reduced in scale, with his daughter Jean reaching out her hand over the table to comfort Archie, and many of the scenes suffered from cutting. The impact of his conversation with Jean about his idea of marrying a young girl was badly muffed by setting it in the open air – Tony Richardson was greedy for every possible ounce of local flavour and we had to watch a merry-go-round with planes on it in the background. With these distractions and subtractions Olivier's performance added up to less than it did in the theatre but the detail of it stood up perfectly to the camera's close-up scrutiny – the thick well-oiled voice, coarsened through shouting in the music hall, the shoulders that wiggled to push points across, even the make-up, which emphasized the mouth and had the hair parted in the middle, making the features look more flabby.

Olivier stayed well in character while singing and dancing, and he showed how Archie's private mannerisms derived from his public performances. He was constantly half-parodying himself in a non-stop act of theatrical camp and the sentences came out like cheap prizes from a fun-fair machine. He was always looking for laughter and approval, with an appeasing tone rising automatically into his voice when he was losing, and gagging compulsively to distract you from something else. He used hand-movements copied not from homosexuals but from imitators of them.

But he built in a clearly defined space between the performance Archie was always giving – not just on the stage – and the feeling behind it. In some scenes, like the love scene with Shirley Anne Field (which does not come into the play) we got a much clearer close-up than the theatre could have given us of the split in his mind. Archie feels quite a lot of emotion, but it is not at all the emotion he is play-acting for the girl. His awareness may be blunted but it is still sharp enough for him to feel hatred for himself and a mixture of pity and contempt for her at the actual moment of making love to her. Things *are* allowed to lie oddly in relation to other things in scenes like this, and the actor's criticism of the character emerges clearly.

He was very good in the pseudo-refinement of the pub scene ('bloody pointless ideeah') and, in building from the moments of talking to Phoebe (his wife) as if talking to a child to moments when his impatience with her had to find at least an indirect outlet. But it was Archie, not Olivier, who was being overdramatic in the broken staggering walk after the telephone conversation with the girl's parents, and, as he backed out of the dressing-room, in the long reproachful look at Billie, his father, who had spilled the beans to them.

The usual answer to questions about the difference between stage and screen performances is that everything has to be reduced in size for the screen. This is misleading because it suggests that all gestures have to be cut down in size, which they do not. It is much more a difference in projecting, filling a space, and in *The Entertainer* Olivier was able to repeat many of the same reactions and movements of his hands and eyes that he had used on stage. The only stage actors who have difficulty in adapting to the screen are the ones who invariably go for the broad effect, who lack precision in their work. Any good stage actor should be able to work effectively on the screen, though a lot of effective screen actors would be unable to fill the space in a theatre.

12 · *THE IMPROVISATION FACTOR*

How far can the film actor sink into a character? Coquelin said that a performance only succeeded when an audience forgot the actor altogether and remembered only the character. But in the cinema how often can you forget that you are watching Greta Garbo or Bette Davis or Rex Harrison or Jeanne Moreau? It is no accident that theatre critics, when they are summing up a plot, use the names of the characters, while film critics use the names of the actors. 'They also hijack the fur pelts that trapper Burt Lancaster is taking to market.' 'Miss Davis loses two lovers to Miss Hopkins and her daughter.'

This encourages a habit which exists already in audiences to react to characters as if they were people. ('I don't like him.' 'Serves her right.' 'Poor woman.') To some extent they do this in the theatre but cinema audiences are more prone to forget even the name of the character (as opposed to the actor) while cinema actors are more prone to turn a part down because it would be bad for their public image.

Jean-Luc Godard, of course, was quick to get some fun out of the fact of having Brigitte Bardot in the cast of *Le Mépris*. While she is on the screen, one of the other characters refers to Bertolt Brecht by his initials. 'B.B.?' she queries quickly.

This is the most blatant but by no means the only instance of Godard's jogging the audience's elbow to make it notice the incompleteness of the identification between the actor and the part.

The interview sequences in *Une Femme Mariée* and *Masculin-Feminin* serve the same purpose with their ambiguity about whether it is the actor or the character who is being interviewed. The ambiguity is at its most complex when Charlotte interviews her lover, Robert, who is an actor, about 'The Theatre and Love': what Bernard Noel (as Robert) says about the actor's attitude to his role could apply to his own attitude to the role he is playing at this moment.

Though Godard is the first director to make full use of Brechtian alienation effects in the cinema – he keeps reminding the audience it is a film they are watching – the cinema has always been closer to Brecht than to Stanislavski: partly because of its fragmentation; partly because of the necessary incompleteness of the actor's identification with the part; and partly because of the camera, with its natural predilection for factuality, recording, documentation. There have been many films (like Renoir's *The River*, from Rumer Godden's flimsy novel) in which the scenery has stolen the show, but in most films, the most photogenic reality is the personality of the star. The story is fiction but the actor is a fact and the performance is often worth filming for itself, irrespective of how well it serves the character, or how feeble the story is. Many films are therefore conceived as vehicles. *Queen Christina* has a grotesquely silly story[1] and surely the most pedestrian dialogue S. N. Behrman ever wrote, but as a vehicle for Garbo it is quite good. Her performance is no more than a display of personality, and Mamoulian must have encouraged this, though he talks of clever directorial devices like using a metronome 'to achieve a rhythmic quality' while the Queen says good-bye to the room in the inn where she has been happy with her lover. Nothing could make this into a real situation. Compared with the scene in *The Cherry Orchard* in which Madam Ranevsky says good-bye to her living-room, it is sheer kitsch. Even in 1933, no audience could have taken the story very seriously, but Garbo is a splendid creature and the film is intensely interesting today, just because it shows her in action. What this amounts to saying is that she found spaces within the rigid framework of scene, situation and Mamoulian's direction where she was free to improvise.

[1] By Salka Viertel and Margaret P. Levine.

There is no characterization – there is no ground for any – but she is fascinating when she behaves quite naturally in doing little things like going out on the balcony to take a deep breath of air.

Cinema must always push the actor in the direction of harnessing his own habits and mannerisms to the performance. Simone Signoret says[1] that she learnt all she knows from Jacques Feyder. When he directed her he used to watch the gestures she made off the set, and draw on them. 'Alors? Et ce geste? Tous les jours vous le faîtes en vous habillant pour partir, pourquois pas maintenant avec le même naturel?'

Jeanne Moreau, though less beautiful than Garbo, is equally arresting as a personality and technically much better as an actress. She, too, contributes something of her own which makes all her films worth watching, however bad they are otherwise. It is worth quoting Peter Brook's account of his experience with her in *Moderato Cantabile*:

Jeanne Moreau is for me the ideal contemporary film actress because she doesn't characterize. She acts in the way Godard films, and with her you are as close as you can be to making a document of an emotion ... Jeanne Moreau works like a medium, through her instincts. She gets a hunch about the character and then some part of her watches the improvisation of that and lets it happen, occasionally intervening a bit like a good technician when, for instance, she wants to be facing the camera, to be at the right angle. But she is guiding the flow of improvisation rather than stating ahead of time what hurdle she wants herself to leap, and the result is that her performance gives you an endless series of tiny surprises. On each take neither you nor she knows exactly what is going to happen . . . And it wasn't actually silence that one was photographing . . . but a look on her face and a tiny movement of her cheek, which to me were valid because she was

[1] *Cinema*, April 1959.

actually *and at that moment* experiencing something which therefore became interesting to look at as an object.[1]

It is misleading though to say that she doesn't characterize. She certainly transforms herself. The desperate blonde gambler in *Baie des Anges*, the unpredictable *gamine fatale* in *Jules et Jim*, the diabolically destructive heroine in *Eve* and the alienated wife in *La Notte* (to take just four of her creations) are very different from each other and her appearance seems to change as much as her rhythm or her manner. This is not a matter of make-up but of the expression on her mobile face. A smile lifts the drooping corners of her mouth into a radiance, and the actual weight of her head seems to vary as she passes from morose heaviness to buoyant animation.

The experience she is having is deep enough and real enough and demonstrable enough to satisfy the newsreel side of the camera's appetite. In bad films her best moments are the ones when she's least restricted by dialogue. There is a clearcut example of this in *Eve* which is a very overrated film, with an overwritten script from a novel by James Hadley Chase, overdirected by Joe Losey and overacted by Stanley Baker. Moreau does her best with a character whose malignity is more motiveless than Iago's and she infuses a very exciting sexuality into some very unexciting lines. But she is only at her best in one scene, her first, in which she hardly speaks a word, and hardly does anything, except take her clothes off to the music of a Billie Holliday record. It is not at all like striptease though. Towelling her wet hair, she is absorbed, quite unprovocatively, in her own body. She reacts much more to the music than to finding a girl's nightdress under the pillow of Tyvian, the man she has come to destroy. Of course she is aware of showing off her body to the camera – of what a good body it is and how well she moves it – but she is also experiencing a genuine animal enjoyment of being inside that body, jumping to make the dress slide off

[1] In an interview in *Sight and Sound*.

and stepping over it to freedom. And this the camera records. When Tyvian finally appears the sexy lethargy is effectively sustained in face of his effusive wordiness. While she says nothing, each intimate appearance of her tongue under the ripe, indulgent upper lip counts for all the more and Gianni di Venanzo's camera slides promisingly over her face as if it might take us right inside her mouth at any minute. She is utterly real and compelling so long as she goes on using just her personality and her technique in close-up and in long shot – the sleek body moving snakelike on the bed. But once ballasted with bad dialogue, she only regains her reality in odd moments of reaction, puffing carelessly at a cigarette or frowning vacuously as Tyvian goes on talking into her silence. With the bad lines and phoney actions, even her voice becomes unreal, affecting a harshness which makes the sound seem dubbed. Not that Moreau is incapable of viciousness on the screen, as she has often shown, but no one could be convincing in the scene of demanding money 'I want to be paid cash' or in taunting Tyvian with another man's flowers. 'In memory of a very happy week-end. Karl.'

Moreau always seems able to infuse a restive activity even into moments of passivity and she combines malleability with a sinewy ability to impose herself. She always makes the most of the transitions from one mood, one pattern of reactions, to another and she can improvise in character within the confines of script and situation. Some of the best scenes in *Jules et Jim* owe their quality to her improvisational contributions. The 'endless series of tiny surprises' is beautifully right for Catherine and beautifully geared to the performances of Oskar Werner and Henri Serre as Jules and Jim. The balance of power between the three of them is constantly changing and Moreau keeps every gradation in every change tinglingly alive.

I believe that this capacity for creative improvisation within the confining context of a script will come to be more and more important as the art of film acting develops. It involves a combination of talent and technique. It involves keeping an element of liberty all the time – giving away just so much to the demands of dialogue, situation and director but reserving the right to be real in the interstices of the fiction. It can be as fatal for the actor to let a pattern be imposed on him as to impose one on himself. His own personality must come into the picture, and, if possible, at least a hint of his attitude to the character.

From this point of view, the best part is the one which leaves the most holes to be filled out. Shirley Knight's part as the racist female sex-murderer in *Dutchman* is a good example. In one sense she is not improvising at all and in another sense she never stops. Each line she speaks is scripted, but what matters more than anything she says is the way she uses everything about herself – body, voice, sexuality, mannerisms – to fill out the lines and irradiate them with suggestive ambiguity. She holds back nothing of herself, but she is in character all the time she is improvising.

She makes every movement expressive, from the first time we see her in a provocative stance against the wall of the underground station and the slinky entrance into the train. There is a luscious sexiness in the way she crosses her legs, chewing on the apple, and in the way she takes her shoe off to loosen the stocking against the toe. She quickly builds up a rhythm of rapid changes of mood, oscillating between friendly teasing banter and cold hostility. Detached and self-absorbed on the surface, appearing to be concentrating on her apple or on studying her legs, she is seductive and then ironic, slightly mocking herself by drawing attention to her own flirtatiousness and then cutting through the young Negro's uncertain reactions to criticize him, directly, insultingly. There is nothing ambiguous about the tone, though the context takes something off the cutting edge.

The rhythm is a biting one with slow progressions and rapid shifts of focus and key. Pensively derogatory, she sizes him up as she goes along, staring shrewdly. She offends him and then reassures him with a hand on his knee – an expertly timed sexual advance to produce the maximum confusion in her victim. But it is never a walk-over for her, although he is a fairly simple type. Partly she seems to be playing to an imaginary audience, working herself up over nothing. But it is all at least *partly* for the effect on him.

She gives every impression of spontaneity in the detail of what she does and the cat and mouse game is an ideal framework for this, with the scope it provides for sexy playfulness. 'Am I exciting you?' With accidental-seeming touches on his body, a light finger on his wrist and suddenly twisting his wrist forcefully, though with laughter bubbling through everything she does, to produce incessant doubt in the man's mind. Is it for real? Is it a game? Is she as worked up as she seems?

What she does is not just ambiguous, it is discordant. She is always doing at least two things at once, playing on two strings of the emotional violin. She is hard to resist when she starts using her tongue to feed him a morsel of his own apple and, finding grey hairs in her head, she becomes pleasingly pathetic. Hints of mental unbalance are planted quite early when her eyes flick sideways at him as she rummages in her bag or puts lipstick on. She always has plenty to do, disguising the fact that she is concentrating on him.

Soon she gets weary with her own initiatives. She has proved her power, so what is the point in going on with the act? There is a definite actress element in her character (which is always an advantage if the character is conscious of it). At one point she pretends to be an actress and she takes obvious pleasure in changing her vocal tone and in mimicking the imagined voices of men he mentions. Then, after a long period of confidence, she is suddenly uncertain of him again when he says his name is Clay. Is he mocking her? She hits back, mocking him.

With a huntress mouth, predatory eyes and predatory fingers – especially later when they cradle his head like claws holding food – she hangs her limbs on her body like fruits ripe for plucking. After a long, well-timed series of alternations between peremptory commands, soft coyness, direct sexual provocations like crossing her legs over his and sudden withdrawals, she comes out with 'Just what are you playing at?'

What makes the performance particularly exciting to watch is the hysteria latent in her vast extrovert energy. Like Brando or Olivier, she might boil over at any minute, and she conveys the impression of not caring what happens to her. Sometimes her face looks as if she is being made love to at that moment. All this she can do to herself, reacting violently when nothing has happened to react to, so long as there is someone there to watch her. She always takes the lead with him, wrapping him into tight embraces, but it is herself that she is enjoying, dreaming, even when she is inveigling him verbally into her fantasy of what they will do after the party. She never listens but she hunches herself into intimacy, a real need to make not contact but impact. It is apt that in the clammy heat of the train, she stays cool while he sweats.

The final lap of sexy aggressiveness starts with her movements in peeling the orange. While she starts the dance through the carriage, we know that release must come in violence. In a wild burst of hysteria she jumps on a seat and holding on to a vertical metal handrail, moves her body as if copulating, fanned into a feverish fury entirely by herself. The weakest part of the film and the performance comes when she stays silent all through his long monologue (she couldn't, at this stage) but it is effective when, knifed by her, he falls on top of her. 'Get this man off me.'

It is very seldom that a film actress gets a chance to go through such a huge gamut of emotion – and of movement – or to give as much of herself as this. Consequently anyone else would have been very different in the part. It would be a hard part for an English actress to play. We have very few girls capable of stripping themselves that bare at that pitch of intensity while preserving that degree of control.

Nevertheless, the performance might provide a cue for actors and actresses over here. It is going to become more important than ever – even when the holes are much smaller than that – to fill them out as truthfully as that, without holding back or hiding. While we are being forced to re-examine the hairline crack where acting stops and reality begins we must explore the no-man's-land of improvisation in character. New freedoms demand new disciplines, new techniques.

///

13 · ACTING FOR TELEVISION

The TV image offers some three million dots per second to the viewer. This mosaic mesh of dots involves the viewer as maker and participant. From these he accepts only a few hundred each instant from which to make an image. The film image in a motion picture theatre offers many more million bits of data per second, and the viewer does not have to make the same drastic reduction of items to form his impression. Put directly and briefly, one has to say of TV that it is a sort of 'spiritual' instrument, with the viewer on the receiving end of a light charge. The TV viewer is the screen and the vanishing point. Hence the extraordinary degree of involvement in the TV experience. The movie viewer remains quite detached and is engaged in looking at the screen. The TV viewer *is* the screen.

This is Marshall McLuhan executing his usual knight's gambit from objective premiss to windy conclusion.[1] And the wind is blowing in the wrong direction, for there are a dozen

[1] Quoted in *Sight and Sound*. Winter 1967.

factors operating against involvement in the television experience. The audience is most often a tiny one of two or three people sitting with the light on. It is possible, I suppose, that unconsciously they are compensating for lack of data but they mostly feel quite free to get up, move around, knit, sew, talk, eat, brew coffee, go out of the room or switch over to another channel. The fact that they do not feel they are paying for what they are watching is no incentive to concentration, and the fact of their not being part of a large group, like a cinema audience, makes it harder to infect them with either excitement or amusement. Television comedy is usually played to a studio audience. This helps both the actors by giving them a response to play to and the small audience in the sitting-room by letting it feel part of a larger pool of spectator reaction. All the same, anyone watching a comedy programme when there are ten other people in the sitting-room will laugh much more than when he is alone, or with one other person.

Eventually, no doubt, we will have bigger television sets but meanwhile the size of the screen is a limitation, as we are reminded each time a film designed for the cinema is shown on television: the image is uncomfortably small. With films and plays designed for television, this shrinking effect has to be avoided, which means that the relationship between the foreground of the picture and the background is quite different from what it is in the cinema. With more than two heads on it, the television screen is crowded, and in scenes involving a large group of characters, where some are speaking and some are not, it is hard for the director to keep the silent ones visually alive. In the cinema it is easy to show them reacting to the foreground action by including them in the picture; on television it is not, and cutting to close-ups of their reactions interrupts the continuity of the foreground action.

Television drama in this country is still in its very early stages, and just as the film started off by drawing on stage techniques, television has started off by drawing on both stage and film techniques. In fact, of course, new techniques in acting, directing and writing need to be evolved specially for the new medium, and in time, no doubt, they will be, but commercial pressures always have a reactionary effect and on television the commercial pressures are pushing actors, directors and writers in the direction of a stodgy naturalism. The endemic fear of losing audiences to another channel encourages a simple, buttonholing style of story-telling and acting. Nothing can be risked that might lead to low ratings. The fourth wall is changed into a screen-shaped keyhole. A Script Services booklet issued by Associated-Rediffusion pronounced

> The object of television acting, in so far as anyone has yet been able to define it, is to make the viewer believe that he is watching something that he is not meant to watch, that he is, in fact, 'dropping in' on something that was going on before he switched on his set and which will continue after he has left.

Who is going to be the Brecht or the Godard who will show that television drama can be even more entertaining when it does not pretend not to be television drama?

In the cinema, many of the devices like jump-cuts which Godard has popularized have the effect of speeding up the action, helping to tell a story faster. Television still works to a tempo which is much too slow, though of course it can not and should not ever become as dependent as filming is on cuts.

Although some of the most successful television plays (like *Up the Junction* and *Cathy Come Home*) could not have been made without telerecording and a good deal of editing, television plays can not for the most part be shot, like films, in short sequences, and the fact that the camera must keep shooting and the actor must keep acting is primarily an advantage. The disadvantage of limited rehearsal time means that all sorts of problems of make-up, costume, props, moves and interpretation have to be sorted out far more quickly than in the theatre or the film studios but the actor does play his part from beginning to end.

So far as timing is concerned, even though the audience may be cutting with the cameras from one character to another, there is far less interference than there is in filming with the rhythm of what the actor actually does. Unless he is working with telerecordings, the director does his cutting and shooting simultaneously. He is probably working almost entirely from his camera plot in the control room, but with the freedom to improvise if he notices something fresh on one of the monitors that he wants to include.

Obviously the results must be cruder than in the cinema, where the editor has time and a cutting-room, but they are also, on the whole, cruder than necessary. The reason for this is that directors stick unnecessarily closely to rule-of-thumb techniques they have been taught. Like this one, formulated by Desmond Davis in *The Grammar of Television Production*.[1]

> Always, when possible, cut on movement within the frame; cut when the subject is in the act of sitting, rising, turning, rather than when the subject is stationary. Even in close-up, prefer a moment for cutting when the head is in motion.

This leads to some very odd results – one of which was described rather well by Robert Vas in *Sight and Sound*:

> A few weeks ago I was watching a television play with a friend, an experienced TV producer. In the climactic scene, the hero visits his rival with the obvious intention of shooting him. He enters the room in a long-shot and stops by the door. The other doesn't see him yet. Tension. He has an air of authority, superiority, that now needs to be intensified. A pause, a static moment of expectancy. The content of the scene, the rhythm of the action,

[1] Desmond Davis, *The Grammar of Television Production*. Barrie and Rockliff.

demands a jump nearer to him, into a closer shot. To under-line his presence. Give it a plus. Indicate a determination to act. Just a bit of plus from the editing department. 'Cut,' I said. I wanted it; I swear the hero wanted it too. But my friend the producer shook his head. 'No,' he said, 'wait until he *moves*. They can cut on movement only.' And truly, the instant the hero whipped out his revolver, there was a cut to a closer shot on the sudden move-ment (so that the change wouldn't show). The cut was hidden all right, but the plus, the push that a deliberate cut would have given, was gone.[1]

Actors vary greatly in the extent to which they are aware – and to which they like to be aware – of technical factors and directors vary in the extent to which they confide in the actors. Some make a point of saying what the cameras will be doing, while others prefer to say as little as possible about their plans for the cameras, knowing that they may well want to change them. One actor may shape up a lot better and another a lot worse than was expected, in which case it can pay off to favour the good one more and the bad one less with the cameras.

Some directors tell actors to carry on exactly as if the cameras were not there. This is bad advice. It is physically impossible to ignore them completely, so it is a strain to attempt to. And while it is a mistake to play into them too directly, it is best, as in filming, for the actor, while involved almost entirely with the situation and the other characters, to have a tiny monitoring corner in his mind where he is roughly aware of the relationship between what he is doing and what the audience will see on their screens.

Acting style and technique on television must be influenced considerably by the fact that audiences may have been watching documentary features and news programmes just before a play begins. Don Taylor, who has directed most of

[1] Robert Vas, article in *Sight and Sound*, Summer 1966.

David Mercer's plays on television, wrote in *Contrast* about one newsreel he saw:

> A short time ago a house was burned down in London. A wife and children died in the flames, and the husband, a railwayman, was brought home from what had started as an ordinary day's work to face complete tragedy. The merciless newsreel cameras were there, and photographed him as he came out of the blackened home after identification of his wife and children. Ironically the family dog was unhurt, and he was carrying it and chucking it gently behind the ear. His face was completely blank. His agony was inward. This piece of film should be seen by any actor who wants to work on television.

Eric Portman once told Harold Lang acting in films had taught him how much too much generalized and inappropriate effort he had formerly employed in the theatre. And of course we still see – not only on the stage but also in films and on television – a lot of unrealistic gesturing, grimacing and heavy breathing which is meant to externalize a strong internal feeling.

A favourite direction of George More O'Ferrall's was 'I don't want to hear what you say. I want to see what you think.' The advantage of the television camera is that it can move right in close and stay in close. Don Taylor describes a close-up which he held for fifteen minutes with only one small movement in David Mercer's *A Climate of Fear*. It was a scene in bed: Frieda Waring was talking to her husband but the actress spoke in a kind of terrified whisper so quietly that the actor lying in bed next to her could not hear and had to be given visual cues.

This kind of effect is much more readily brought off on television than in any other medium. A good example of the way cinema is predisposed to miss this kind of chance is provided by the closing scene in Tennessee Williams's *Suddenly Last Summer*. The play ends with a long narrative from

Catharine, who describes how Sebastian Venable, the poet, was killed last summer in Cabeza de Lobo. This is the key speech of the play: everything else leads up to it and the whole action focuses on the story that gets told in it. The reason Sebastian's mother wants a lobotomy to be performed on Catharine is to prevent her from passing it on to other people. There are a lot of interruptions, questions and promptings from the doctor, but they are not important and for eight pages of the script, Catharine's narrative is all that matters. How Sebastian bought her a swimsuit that went transparent in water so that she would involuntarily be procuring for him. How the naked beggar children cried out for bread at the barbed wire fence outside the restaurant and serenaded the diners with tin-cans and improvised cymbals. How Sebastian got the waiters to drive them away with clubs and skillets. How they pursued Sebastian up the hill while Catharine ran the other way shouting for help, and how she came back to find that he was dead, stripped naked, and that parts of his body had been torn or cut away, and eaten. The speech is a *tour de force* in the writing and it should be a *tour de force* in the performance, as it was when Patricia Neal played it superbly at the Arts Theatre.

The point is that the force of the passage does not in the least depend on visual effects. Nothing is happening on stage except that she is talking out what she remembers. The theatrical impact depends on the words and the rhythms and the tension and the pictures that they create in the audience's mind. On television this could be done even better than it could in the theatre because most of the stage picture is irrelevant in this scene and the television camera could close right in, as it did in *A Climate of Fear*, to hold the actress relentlessly in a close-up while she undergoes the strain of remembering and reliving the experience.

Theoretically, this could also be done on film, but it never would be. Audiences are conditioned to expect plenty of visual variety, a succession of edited sequences, not a sustained close-up on a monologue. This is a problem that has bedevilled so many Shakespeare films. What happened in the film of *Suddenly Last Summer* was that flashbacks were inter-cut into the narrative, so that the effect no longer depended on the words Elizabeth Taylor was speaking or the way she was speaking them. It was the director, not the actress or the writer, who was creating the pictures.

If the visual image is the prime factor in the cinema, as the spoken word is in the theatre, television represents a very useful halfway house. Its immediate appeal is visual but it does not depend primarily on a montage of edited sequences and, as in the theatre, it is the script, not the director, that determines the sequence and the structure. But it is striking that the moments in a television play which communicate most are often the moments in which the characters are saying least. Silences, glances, hesitations, moments where understanding or a failure of understanding can be made clear to the viewer without any dialogue are far more power-ful pieces of vocabulary than the average television play-wright realizes. He thinks too much in terms of developing his story-line through dialogue and not sufficiently in terms of a succession of images on a screen. This is one of the factors which are making it difficult to evolve a technique of acting which is generically appropriate to television.

If I cite the BBC's production of Simon Gray's *Spoiled*[1] as an example, it is not because it is a bad one. But it is a clear one. The actors (Michael Craig, Simon Ward, Elizabeth Shepherd and Carmel McSharry) and the director (Waris Hussein) built up in the spaces between the words very promising and interesting hints about the areas in the characters' lives where they were not articulate about what was going on, or even conscious of it. What was particularly clear, and touching, was the way they were reaching out to each other, wanting to make contact, and to help, but failing, and doing harm. The shy, fatherless, anxiety-ridden boy who

[1] August 1968.

keeps failing his exam (Simon Ward) has started making noises in his sleep and his stupid, well-meaning, ultra-religious mother (Carmel McSharry) thinks she is helping when she tells him that it is the devils in him trying to get out. But in her exchanges of glances with him in the bedside scene, there are hints of the panicky feeling each has of having let the other down. Much as they want to make contact with each other, neither of them is capable of either finding the right words or finding the courage to reach out without words.

Certainly the cues for this moment and the others like it are all in Simon Gray's script, but the silences do not quite integrate with the dialogue. They raise the production to a higher level than could have been achieved by relying more fully on the scripted lines, but at the same time they pose questions which neither the words nor the action could answer. I felt that if Simon Gray had had the chance of rewriting his play after he had seen how much the actors could get across in silence, he could have come up with a more honest and penetrating script.

The subject is one which lends itself very well to treatment of this sort. The revulsion that the teacher (Michael Craig) feels from his seven-month pregnant wife (Elizabeth Shepherd) is clear enough and it is obvious that this intensifies his natural and perfectly healthy fondness for the boy, whom he is coaching. He helps to build up his confidence and, unlike anyone else, he helps him to feel that emotional problems *can* be dragged out into the daylight of conversation. But after taking advantage of the boy's response to make love to him once, he withdraws completely, evading contact and leaving his bewildered, fragile victim to find his own way out of the emotional mess. But it is not only the boy who is let down by the sudden drying up of the teacher's flow of talk – it is the whole play. The build-up of the relationship promised a different kind of resolution. It is clear that the boy will now become still more withdrawn and neurotic but his predicament needs a fuller, more sympathetic treatment, which could have been achieved if Simon Gray had known how to exploit the actors and the medium more fully without the aid of dialogue.

Writers will only learn this if experiments are made which involve them in quite different relationships with actors and directors. And this is the only way in which actors can find out how to make more of the silent moments that are possible on television and how to integrate them better with the dialogue. (Possibly, in the transition phase at least, improvised dialogue should be used more as a bridge between silences, which are necessarily improvisational, and dialogue, which is not.) Television acting will only come into its own when a technique is evolved which is wholly appropriate to the medium, cashing in on all the opportunities it offers and exploiting its differences from both theatre and film.

Can we find any clues in past television performances about the lines on which this technique might develop? There is one clue in the best acting performance I have seen on television – Judi Dench's in John Hopkins's quartet of television plays *Talking to a Stranger*.

Judi Dench's part was written specially for her and the character, Terry, speaks the same flip language she speaks herself. (This helps rather in the way that it helped Simone Signoret to be directed into making use of her own gestures.) Terry is the victim of an over-protective father. As an adolescent she has been vulnerable because she has expected the same kind of lovingness from every other man and as an adult she is still prey to vestiges of the old vulnerableness but vindictive now, and bitter, because she has been hurt so often. She defends herself either too fiercely or not at all. She has never learnt – and never will – the balance. Judi Dench implicitly suggests (as John Hopkins does in his script) that many daughters are cruel to many fathers (and to men in general) in more or less this way for more or less these reasons and at the same time she makes the emotion very much her own, torturing it out of her own extraordinary mixture of hardness and softness. She has the attractively vulnerable face of a grown-up baby and a voice which holds a precarious balance between authoritative toughness and overwhelming self-pity. She can change her tone instantly from lashing bitterness to pathetic pleading. She can dominate easily, as she does in the scene with Jess, her flat-mate, but whether she is in command or out of control, she produces a tension that hints at a dozen contradictory things, all interesting, going on under the surface. Her face is never blank, like the railwayman's, but it never entirely corresponds to the emotion that she convinces herself she is feeling. In both the tirades of resentful mockery in the family scenes and the painful essays in reconstructing the past with Alan, her brother, she gives enough hints of the underlying muddle and agony, the non-stop wrestling match that goes on inside herself between the victim and the aggressor. Like Laurence Olivier as Archie Rice, but in a completely different way, she persuades us that the self-dramatization is a necessary shield for the desperateness.

John Hopkins's script is ideal for television but highly untypical of what is normally done on it. Any unknown playwright submitting a synopsis for a play like any one of these four would not even have it considered, because the situation is so static and there is a high ratio of dialogue to action. But it is precisely this that gives the actors space to explore their characters and situations and it is this sort of microscopic exploration that is ideal for the television close-up. Most television scripts almost force the actors into cliché with the kind of dialogue and action that necessitates shortcuts in the characterization.

The script of *Talking to a Stranger* does not leave holes for the actors in the same way that LeRoy Jones's script does in *Dutchman*. At the same time there is a lot in Judi Dench's performance that can only be described as improvisational, and which explores her own temperament and personality as Jeanne Moreau does and as Shirley Knight does in *Dutchman*. Although the words are more important than they can be in a film, a great deal depends on moods and the transitions between them. Another actress would have created a totally different characterization. It is no accident that the three examples I have picked of this kind of acting are all women, for women articulate mood and mood-changes more readily, but the argument holds good for men.

A television camera has just as much of a newsreel appetite as a film camera and the 'endless series of tiny surprises' that Judi Dench produced were well worth documenting. Rehearsal time must have been taken up very largely by getting familiar with the words and the moves, for it is a huge part and there could not possibly have been time for detailed planning of all the emotional gear-changes. But those reactions in her eyes, now glinting with anger, now flooding with pain, and the choked modulations in the husky agonized voice must have been all the better for not being better rehearsed.

The point I have been leading up to is that this sort of improvisation ought to be basic to television acting. Both the documentary nature of the medium and the inevitable shortness of rehearsal time support this conclusion. The actor's performance should be the news that the camera is recording and his feelings at the moment, including his feelings about the character and the situation, can legitimately enter into the picture. Very few performances on television or film succeed in integrating the critical attitude that Brecht demanded or even in doing what Claire Trevor did in *Stagecoach* – holding back from total submergence in a way that makes it possible to give simultaneous indications of an inner life and a critical attitude. But the goal should be to channel spontaneity into helping in these two ways. This is how to capitalize on the inevitable fact that in films and television, the actor cannot disappear into the role.

As things are, a lot of good actors work on television but produce very few good performances. Much of the trouble stems from the fact that the programme planners seem to be unaware that there is – or could be – such a thing as television acting. A lot of careful thought goes into planning programmes of television drama but nobody attempts any basic thinking about the acting. It is tacitly assumed that there is only one technique of acting.

In their starry, prestige production of *Twelfth Night*, shot in 1968, A.T.V. were quite happy to leave the casting entirely in the hands of a director (John Dexter) who had no experience of television, and to dichotomize the production by letting him direct the actors while someone else (John Sichel) directed the cameras. It is a colour production which will not be screened until A.T.V. can show it in colour, so I cannot yet judge the results,[1] but the principle is wrong. With Shakespeare, as with any other playwright, television offers certain advantages and suffers from certain limitations which are unlike those of any other medium. There is technique both in exploiting the advantages and in turning the limitations to advantage. Joan Plowright, who plays Viola, and Sir Alec Guinness, who plays Malvolio, are both subtle and precise enough in their work to be capable of giving excellent performances on television, but they are both new to the medium and to put them in the hands of a director who is also new to it is an experiment of the wrong kind, at a time when there is a crying need for experiments of the right kind to be made – the kind which will lead to evolving a technique of television acting.

Much of what passes for acting in run-of-the-mill productions is not acting at all. As in the cinema, the thrillers depend largely on spectacle, stunts and fights, while the dialogue, such as it is, demands very little from the actors beyond mechanically casual villainy and mechanically deadpan heroism. Underplaying is taken to such an extreme that

[1] Written in autumn, 1968.

it becomes a formula. It is not just the lines that are 'thrown away', it is everything else too. The balance breaks down, as if the only alternative to underplaying were overplaying. When Patrick McGoohan played Ibsen's Brand at the Lyric, Hammersmith in 1959, he was a very good actor, but all those years of *Danger Man* and *The Prisoner* have had a disastrous effect on his technique. In the relatively few scenes which require the actors to act, he is now liable to impose emotion fiercely from the outside, clenching his voice into a near-shout, like a parody of Olivier at his worst.

There are also a lot of comedy programmes on television which use actors without requiring them to act. *All Gas and Gaiters* was a particularly inane example with William Mervyn, Robertson Hare and Derek Nimmo all getting laughs out of personal mannerisms and feeble situation comedy. Even in much better serials and series, like *Steptoe and Son*, the basic characterizations tend to get pushed into vaudeville coarseness of texture. Far the best piece of acting in television comedy has come from Warren Mitchell as Alf Garnett in *Till Death Do Us Part* and the curious thing here is that for most people the actor has totally disappeared into the character. Nobody wrote about Warren Mitchell's achievement in creating a character so forceful and so different from himself. Even quite intelligent critics wrote as if Alf Garnett existed in his own right.

This is all a great pity and a great waste, for television is a new medium with an enormous potential not only for forging a new technique of acting but for educating a public to appreciate it. Acting could become a more popular art than it has ever been before. Obviously it is too much to hope that every housewife and every engineer will become as knowledgeable and enthusiastic about acting as an aficionado about bull-fighting, but television is better equipped than any other medium for demonstrating to the public at large that the more it understands about acting, the more it will enjoy it.

14 · *NOT A CONCLUSION*

Even if this had been a much longer book, it could not have been a conclusive one. Acting technique can only be evolved on the stage and in the film and television studios. All a book can do is collate examples, analyse, criticize, theorize, make suggestions and perhaps dispel a little of the vagueness that surrounds so much discussion of acting.

Some actors still behave as though it were useless and rather improper to talk about technique at all. This coyness was fairly harmless in the days of the actor managers. Sir Donald Wolfit held that there was only room for one creative performance in any production – all the others had to be fitted in around it. But today everybody is expected to adapt to everybody else and it ought to be self-evident that they cannot do that nearly so well if they only know what everybody else is doing, not how they are doing it.

In theatres like the National and the Royal Shakespeare and the better repertories which keep a permanent company, everybody gets more or less used to everybody else's way of working, but in most stage productions and in films and television plays, the director picks the actors he wants without any thought for their methods of working or their compatibility. It is left to them to make hasty adaptations to each other and to his demands on them, often knowing that what they are doing is wrong, but also knowing that compromise is necessary to achieve a presentable result within the given time. Compromise is always necessary, but there are degrees beyond which it is artistically damaging. Altogether acting suffers far too much from ad hoc solutions.

Theory is only valuable in so far as it helps to monitor practice, but current practice suffers seriously from the surrounding atmosphere of vagueness about technique. It is a vicious circle of vagueness which starts in the acting world itself and spreads far beyond it. While actors and directors are mostly indefinite about what it is that they are doing, critics and audiences are vague about what they are reacting to and an uninformed audience, incapable of appreciating the finer points of a performance, has a dulling effect on that performance. For an audience that listens to Alf Garnett and watches the Coronation Street gossips as if they were real people, all that matters is the identification, and the more naturalistic the better. Once a character is established, all the actor has to do is to go on living as consistently and uncritically as possible inside his skin, trying not to think, trying not to make the audience think. Nothing comes to matter except the billing, the salary, the length of the contract and the ratings. So the actor gives up art for business.

In films and television, the same pattern is being repeated again and again on different levels. Patrick McGoohan has his own company to make his own films. So has Albert Finney, though he does not work exclusively for it. But Peter O'Toole, even in 1963, was already devoting most of his time to the film business and he only gave a dozen performances as Hamlet in our National Theatre's opening production. Portrait of the artist as young tycoon.

The only way that acting could go back to being an art is through a genuine spread of consciousness about what acting is. If this can happen, it will not be as the result of any initiative taken by any individual, or any group. It will be a gradual movement, a process. I would like to end by trying to define the form I think it could take, but I can only do this by repeating points I have made already.

1. We need a better vocabulary. This cannot be arrived at just by sitting down and making it up. It can only be evolved out of coherent discussions about acting, not only in the rehearsal rooms and the studios but on

television and in the newspapers. The present reviewing system is inadequate. Even a magnificent performance like Sir Laurence Olivier's in *The Dance of Death* gets summed up in two or three sentences of a notice devoted partly to the play, partly to the production and partly to the other performances.

2. Actors, directors, producers, casting directors and programme planners all need to become more conscious of the different technical demands that the three media make.

3. Characterization needs to get beyond Zolaesque naturalism, photographic portraiture and the off-stage biography approach. New principles of selecting details need to be evolved, and above all new ways of combining realistic with non-realistic elements.

4. Stanislavski and Brecht will both go on leaving traces in our theatrical bloodstream for a long time to come, but we need to be more conscious of our bearings in relation to them and of their limitations as guides to problems which are no longer the same as the ones they were involved with. Stanislavski did not die till 1938 but his ideas mostly belong to the nineteenth century. Brecht did not die till 1956 but the main part of his theorizing was done in the Twenties and Thirties. Neither of them took much account of films and television which not only employ most of our actors for most of the time but have an influence on stage style and stage technique.

5. We need to be much clearer about what the actor is doing with the part of himself that does not disappear into the role.

6. The frontier where acting starts and stops needs to be investigated more thoroughly.

7. We need to become more conscious about the relationship between the planned elements in a performance and the improvised elements.

8. The possibilities and the difficulties of improvising in character need to be studied more.

9. We need to become more aware of the influence that modern playwrights are having on acting style in both modern and not-so-modern plays, and the influence should be encouraged.

10. Acting needs to catch up with the other arts, both creative and interpretative, and to be more open to influence from current movements inside them.

11. Audiences must gradually be educated to appreciate good acting and to resent it when they are fobbed off with clichés.

12. We need drama schools to adjust better to the idea that there is more than one technique of acting to be taught.

13. We need a studio where professionals can do exercises to stave off the technical rigor mortis that type-casting and underplaying to a formula induces.

14. We need more experiments in production like Peter Brook's *Oedipus* and Ingmar Bergman's *Hedda Gabler* in which an old play gets updated and has the tempo of its exposition accelerated.

15. We need studios and experimental plays and films and television productions which involve the writer in different relationships with the actor, so as to leave him free in areas where he is usually bound and to bind him in areas where he is usually left free.

16. In films and television, as on the stage, supporting actors could contribute far more than they are currently being allowed to contribute. We need to develop techniques to exploit them properly. This could only result – but it could hardly fail to result – from a general spread of consciousness about technique.

17. We need to work towards a new balance between body-movement and speech.

APPENDIX I · PERFORMANCES

CHAPTER 2

CHAPTER 6

CHAPTER 7

the Queen's in 1967 and Alla Tarassova in the Moscow
Art Theatre's season at Sadlers Wells in 1951

p. 88   Paul Scofield as Charles Dyer in Charles Dyer's *Staircase*
at the Aldwych in 1966
Ekkehard Schall as Arturo Ui in Brecht's *The Resistible
Rise of Arturo Ui* in 1958
Patrick Wymark as the Judge in John Mortimer's *The
Judge* at the Cambridge in 1967

CHAPTER 8

p. 92   John Gielgud as Oedipus and Irene Worth as Jocasta in
Seneca's *Oedipus* adapted by Ted Hughes at the Old Vic
in 1968

p. 94   Colin Blakely as Creon, Frank Wylie as Tiresias and
Louise Purnell as Manto

p. 95   Ronald Pickup as the Messenger

CHAPTER 9

p. 103 Brigitte Bardot in Roger Vadim's *Et Dieu Créa la Femme*,
1956

p. 104 Edward G. Robinson as Johnny Rocco in John Huston's
Key Largo, 1948

p. 106 Janet Leigh in Hitchcock's *Psycho*, 1960

p. 108 Albert Finney as Arthur in Karel Reisz's *Saturday Night
and Sunday Morning*, 1960

p. 109 Hugh Griffith as Squire Western in Tony Richardson's
Tom Jones, 1963

p. 111 Marilyn Monroe in Laurence Olivier's *The Prince and the
Showgirl*, 1957
John Gielgud as Henry IV in Orson Welles's *The Chimes
at Midnight*, 1965

p. 112 Marlene Dietrich as Lola-Lola in Joseph von Sternberg's
The Blue Angel, 1930
Emil Jannings in *The Blue Angel* and in F. W. Murnau's
The Last Laugh, 1924

p. 113 Louise Brooks as Lulu in Pabst's *Pandora's Box*, 1928, and
his *The Loves of Jeanne Ney*, 1927

p. 114   Marlene Dietrich as Frenchie in George Marshall's *Destry Rides Again*, 1939
Garbo in Mamoulian's *Queen Christina*, 1933
Al Jolson as Jackie in Alan Crosland's *The Jazz Singer*, 1927

CHAPTER 10

p. 117   Claude Laydu in Bresson's *Le Journal d'un Curé de Campagne*, 1950
Nadine Nortier in his *Mouchette*, 1967

p. 118   Lamberto Maggiorani as the Father and Enzo Staiola as the Boy in De Sica's *Bicycle Thief*, 1948
Maria Pia Casilio in his *Umberto D*, 1952

p. 121   Lillian Gish as Elsie, Henry B. Walthall as Ben and Mae Marsh as Flora in Griffith's *The Birth of a Nation*, 1915

p. 122   George Bancroft as Bull Weed and Clive Brook as Rolls Royce in von Sternberg's *Underworld*, 1927
Douglas Fairbanks (Senior) in F. Richard Jones's *The Gaucho*, 1928, and Lupe Velez as the Mountain Girl

p. 123   James Cagney as Tom Powers in William Wellman's *Public Enemy*, 1931
John Gilbert as Antonio in *Queen Christina*
J. Farrell McDonald as Corporal Casey in John Ford's *The Iron Horse*, 1924

p. 124   Andy Devine as Buck, George Bancroft as Curly, Claire Trevor as Dallas, Thomas Mitchell as Doc Boone, Donald Meek as Peacock, John Carradine as Hatfield, Berton Churchill as Gatewood, John Wayne as Ringo and Louise Platt as Lucy in John Ford's *Stagecoach*, 1939

p. 126   Orson Welles as *Citizen Kane*, 1940
Dorothy Comingore as Susan, George Coulouris as Thatcher

p. 127   Everett Sloane as Mr Bernstein and Joseph Cotten as Jedediah.
Noel Coward, Celia Johnson, John Mills, Bernard Miles and Richard Attenborough in Noel Coward's *In Which We Serve*, co-directed with David Lean, 1942

APPENDIX II · REFERENCES TO
BOOKS AND MAGAZINES

CHAPTER 1

p. 6   Paul Scofield, interview in *The Player*, Lillian and Helen
         Ross, Simon and Schuster, 1962

p. 9   *Strasberg at the Actors' Studio* (tape-recorded sessions), ed.
         Robert H. Hethmon, Cape, 1966

p. 10   Kierkegaard, *Crisis in the Life of an Actress*, Collins, 1967

p. 11   Robert Brustein, *Seasons of Discontent*, Cape, 1966

p. 13   George Cukor, interview in *Double Exposure*, Delacorte
         Press, New York, 1966

p. 16   Boris E. Zhakava, *Principles of Directing*, quoted in
         Directing the Play, ed. Toby Cole and Helen Krich Chinoy,
         Crown, 1949
         'Meyerhold Speaks', article in *Encore* No. 48
         Alec Guinness, Kenneth Tynan, Rockcliff, 1953.

CHAPTER 2

p. 19   Richard Flecknoe, *The Acting of Richard Burbage* (1664),
         quoted by E. K. Chambers in *The Elizabethan Stage*,
         O.U.P., 1923

p. 20   Sarah Bernhardt, *The Art of the Theatre*, Bles, 1924

p. 21   Diderot, *The Paradox of Acting* (1773), translated by W.
         H. Pollock, Chatto and Windus, 1883

p. 22   Mrs Siddons: quoted in *Actors on Acting*, edited by Toby
         Cole and Helen Krich Chinoy, Crown, 1949
         (This book was a valuable source for quotations in this
         chapter.)

p. 23   G. H. Lewes, *On Actors and the Art of Acting*
         Benoit Constant Coquelin, 'Acting and Actors' article in
         Harpers New Monthly Magazine, May 1887, reprinted in
         Actors on Acting, ed. Toby Cole and Helen Krich Chinoy

p. 23 Salvini, 'Some Views on Acting', article in *Theatre Workshop*, October 1936

p. 24 William Archer, *Masks or Faces? A Study in the Psychology of Acting*, Longmans, 1885

p. 25 Stanislavski, *An Actor Prepares*, Bles, 1937

CHAPTER 3

p. 28 Laurence Olivier, Edith Evans and Sybil Thorndike, interviews in *Great Acting*. Ed. Hal Burton, BBC Publications, 1967

p. 30 Eugène Ionesco, Preface to *Les Possédés*, adapted from Dostoevski by Akakia Viala and Nicolas Bataille, Editions Emile-Paul, 1959. Quoted in Martin Esslin, *The Theatre of the Absurd*, Eyre and Spottiswoode, 1962 Laurence Olivier, interview in *Great Acting*

p. 33 *Stanislavski on the Art of the Stage*, translated with an introductory essay by David Magarshack, Faber, 1950

p. 34 Stanislavski, *My Life in Art*, Bles, 1924

p. 35 Vanessa Redgrave, television interview reprinted in *The Listener*, 3rd August 1967

p. 36 Stanislavski, *Building a Character*, Max Reinhardt, 1950

CHAPTER 4

p. 37 *Stanislavski on the Art of the Stage*

p. 38 *My Life in Art*

p. 40 *My Life in Art* *The Seagull Produced by Stanislavski*, production score edited by Professor Balukhaty, Dobson, 1952

p. 42 *My Life in Art*

p. 43 *Stanislavski on the Art of the Stage* Stanislavski, *An Actor Prepares*, Bles, 1937

p. 45 Strindberg, Preface to *Miss Julie* translated by Edwin Björkman

p. 46 *An Actor Prepares*

p. 47 Geraldine Page, interview in *The Player*, Lillian and Helen Ross, Simon and Schuster, 1962

CHAPTER 5

p. 47 ⎱
p. 48 ⎰   *Brecht on Theatre*, translated and edited by John Willett,
p. 50 ⎰   Methuen, 1964

p. 52   Angelika Hurwicz, interview in *Theaterarbeit*, a Berliner
Ensemble publication, 1952

p. 54   Helene Weigel, interview in *Theaterarbeit*

p. 60   Michael Redgrave, *Mask or Face*, Heinemann Educational Books, 1958
John Gielgud directs Richard Burton in Hamlet, a journal
of rehearsals, ed. Richard Sterne, Heinemann Educational Books, 1968

p. 61   John Gielgud, *Stage Directions*, Heinemann Educational
Books, 1963

p. 63   Ronald Hayman, 'A Last Interview with Brecht', The
London Magazine, November 1956

CHAPTER 6

p. 66   A. C. Bradley, *Shakespearean Tragedy*, Macmillan, 1904

p. 67   F. R. Leavis, 'Diabolic Intellect and the Noble Hero' in
The Common Pursuit, Chatto and Windus, 1952

p. 73   Kenneth Haigh in a public discussion reprinted in *Encore*
No. 43
Meyerhold quoted in Professor S. D. Balukhaty,
The Seagull Produced by Stanislavski, Dobson, 1952

p. 74   Richard Boleslavski, *The First Six Lessons in Acting*,
Dobson, 1949

p. 75   Peter Brook in the public discussion reprinted in *Encore*
No. 43
Albert Finney, television interview reprinted in *The
Listener*, August 24, 1967

CHAPTER 7

p. 79   Coquelin, 'Acting and Actors', article in *Harpers New
Monthly Magazine*, May 1887

p. 80   *Strasberg at the Actors' Studio*, ed. Robert H. Hethmon, Cape, 1966

p. 82   Robert Lewis, 'Would you please talk to those people', interview in the *Tulane Drama Review*. Vol. 9 No. 2, Winter 1964

CHAPTER 8

p. 91   Stanislavski, *Building a Character*, Max Reinhardt, 1950
            Michael Murray, 'Diary of a Small Part Actor', article in *Encore* No. 42

p. 98   Antonin Artaud, *The Theatre and Its Double*, translated by Mary Caroline Richards, Grove Press, 1958

p. 100   Jerzy Grotowski, *Towards a Poor Theatre*, Odin Teatrets Forlag, 1968

CHAPTER 9

p. 104   James Agee, article on John Huston, published in *Life* September 18, 1950, reprinted in *James Agee on Film*, Peter Owen, 1963

p. 108   Albert Finney, television interview reprinted in *The Listener*, August 24, 1967

p. 109   Pudovkin, *Film Technique and Film Acting*, 1933. Vision, 1948

p. 110   Alain Resnais, an interview from *Cahiers du Cinéma* reprinted in *Films and Filming*, February 1962

p. 111   Roger Hudson, *Sight and Sound*, Spring 1966

p. 112   John Gielgud, interview in *Great Acting*, BBC Publications, 1967

p. 113   Siegfried Kracauer, *From Caligari to Hitler*, Dobson, 1947
            Louise Brooks, from an article in *Positif* No. 75, May 1966, quoted in John Kobal, *Marlene Dietrich*, Studio Vista

p. 115   Stanislavski, *Building a Character*, Max Reinhardt, 1950

CHAPTER 10

p. 115   Eisenstein, article in *Sight and Sound*

p. 116   David Thomson, *Movie Man*, Secker and Warburg, 1967

p. 117   Bresson, interview with Jean-Luc Godard in *Cahiers du Cinéma*

p. 118   De Sica, interview in *Sight and Sound*, April 1950

p. 120   John Ford, interview in *John Ford* by Peter Bogdanovich, Studio Vista

CHAPTER 11

p. 133   David Thomson, *Movie Man*, Secker and Warburg, 1967

p. 135   Antonioni, an interview in *Film Culture*, Nos. 22–3, Summer 1961

p. 139   Vanessa Redgrave, television interview, reprinted in *The Listener*, August 3, 1967

p. 142   David Thomson, *Movie Man*

CHAPTER 12

p. 148   Peter Brook, interview in *Sight and Sound*

CHAPTER 13

p. 153   Marshall McLuhan quoted in *Sight and Sound*, Winter 1967

p. 156   Desmond Davis, *The Grammar of Television Production*, Barrie and Rockliff, 1960

p. 157   Robert Vas in *Sight and Sound*, Summer 1966

p. 158   Don Taylor, article in *Contrast*, Spring 1964

INDEX